Gerald Priestland

YOURS FAITHFULLY

Collected Radio Talks

By arrangement with the
British Broadcasting Corporation

COLLINS
Fount Paperbacks

First published by Fount Paperbacks 1979

Made and printed in Great Britain by
William Collins Sons & Co Ltd, Glasgow

A.M.G.D.

Contents

Introduction

It is a strange sensation to patrol the borderland between journalism and religion. You may tell people it is just like any other kind of hack-work, but it is not. A Christian journalist is constantly tugged to and fro between objectivity and commitment. Furthermore, your audience/readers/viewers take the subject a great deal more seriously than they do politics, diplomacy or economics, and they write in saying so. I reported earth-shaking events in Washington for seven years without getting more than a dozen letters all the time. Now, as the B.B.C.'s Religious Affairs Correspondent, I feel uneasy if I don't get that many letters a day. That is as it should be. A broadcaster should know whom he is talking to. And if they tell him he is speaking to their condition, that makes the job much more worthwhile than the salary by itself does.

As I have tried to make clear, I am not an ordained minister and have no training in theology whatsoever. I am an ecumenical Quaker, a Christian in the sense that I know Jesus is Lord, and I am quite certain that the job I am doing now is the most worthwhile I have ever done in thirty years of broadcasting. Perhaps it is the result of advancing age and experience, but I find more to fascinate me in the eternal issues of the meaning of life, salvation and death than I ever did in the merry-go-round of people demanding things and hitting each other if they did not get them. Not that the churches stay aloof from such issues. They have, as they have always had, a finger in every pie. People who say the Church should keep out of politics usually mean it should only concern itself with *their* brand of politics. My beat is one of infinite variety, crowded with personalities. What more could a journalist ask for?

I took the beat (or diocese?) over from that robust church journalist Douglas Brown – whom God preserve.

Among my inheritance was a five-minute Saturday talk-spot which Douglas had called *Outlook*. Realizing that I could not hope to match Douglas's style and knowledge, I renamed it *Yours Faithfully*. What follows are essentially transcripts drawn from the first eighteen months of the series, between January 1977 and July 1978. I offer them with the following warnings and qualifications.

The scripts have been very slightly altered here and there, simply to allow for the difference between something designed to be performed by the author (taking advantage of vocal inflexion and emphasis) and the same thing presented for silent study by an unknown reader.

Next, I hope nobody will overemphasize the importance of these little essays. I have already explained that I am nothing more than a scribbler with an interest in religion, and I hope nobody will imagine that what I say compares in importance with what the working minister, priest or elder actually does pastorally for the greater glory of God.

Finally, I must express my gratitude to the B.B.C. – my employers for almost thirty years – for allowing me to print these talks and for giving me the opportunity to write them in the first place. My superiors, John Lang and Michael Mayne of the Religious Broadcasting Department, have been extremely tolerant in allowing me to air all kinds of outrageous (but I trust appropriately 'balanced') points of view. But I think I should make it clear that such views are not necessarily theirs or the B.B.C.'s (which is said to have no views, and indeed it is often hard to conceive of a B.B.C. that might have views) or, for that matter, even my own views. After so many years of caution, balance and 'on the one hand black but on the other white', one begins to find it very difficult to make up one's mind about anything.

GERALD PRIESTLAND

Dear Listener

15 January 1977

So where is Douglas Brown whose voice, with the texture of an old oak door, has been the joy of listeners to this spot over the past ten years?

I am glad to say that Douglas is alive and well and living in his beloved East Anglia. Although this is laughingly called 'retirement', Douglas remains fully engaged in the world of religious affairs, a world he has watched over, on the B.B.C.'s behalf, for more than a quarter of a century. Coalminers may have had enough at sixty, but not our Douglas. We have not by any means heard the last of him. He certainly has my invitation to this microphone whenever my own voice or inspiration gives way. I hope he will forgive my changing the title of the programme from *Outlook*, but *Outlook* without Douglas Brown would have been rather like *Letter from America* without Alistair Cooke: it was essentially 'The Douglas Brown Show'.

But it was not just inspiration, or even the quality of his voice, that made Douglas so valued a communicator for the church people of Britain – it was sheer, thorough knowledge. And I had better confess, before it becomes all too obvious, that in succeeding Douglas as Religious Affairs Correspondent of the B.B.C. I do not pretend to compete with that depth of knowledge. Give me, perhaps, another ten years – and by that time I shall have retired, too. Even then, I doubt if I shall have acquired Douglas's discretion, or his touch with subtleties. Followers of the religious press will be aware how highly he is regarded among the churches, right across the board – from the Evangelical *Crusade* to the *Catholic Herald*, you won't find a hard word. (You may find one or two hesitations about *my* appointment, though, and I am not really surprised at that.)

For while Douglas Brown is a traditional, ritual-loving High Anglican, I happen to be a member of that odd bunch, the Society of Friends, the Quakers. This will not, I trust, affect my objectivity any more than Douglas's Anglo-Catholicism affected his. The days are long past when Quakers could be accounted a melancholy, killjoy sect that drew back in horror from the contamination of other Christians. I happen to believe, in the wake of Hans Küng, that to be Christian is to be truly human to the full. Still, I thought it might be worth stating frankly how I see my particular window affecting the view I get.

The other day, in a talk on the B.B.C. World Service, I was asked for a 'manifesto'. I repeated what I reckon has to be the motto of any fallible newsman: I'll do my best to publish the truth; I'm darned sure it won't be the whole truth; it'll be a miracle if it's nothing but the truth. In the course of pursuing that truth I shall try (as George Fox, the Quaker founder, put it) to walk cheerfully through the world, answering that of God in every man; to keep my mind open to new light, from whatever quarter it may arise; and to maintain communication (a former age would have said, without ambiguity, intercourse) as the only alternative to violence and war.

So if I see myself as an ecumenical, Jesus-centred Quaker, I am still a Quaker journalist, far too absorbed by this poetic, fascinating and deeply human area of religion to feel inclined to dismiss lightly other views of it. In a way, becoming Religious Affairs Correspondent is just a logical extension of the Foreign Correspondent's work that I have done for so long. Here we go again, parachuting into new territory – territory that I have in fact visited superficially in the past, where I speak a little of the language and which, above all, I like and begin to feel at home in.

Religious Affairs is a territory which I see as a very broad one, by no means restricted to Christianity. For me, it takes in not only the worship, thought and activities of the various religious traditions now to be found in Britain, but also those beliefs and ideas which have a religious interpretation or dimension to them, and the religious concerns and interests of people who may be on the fringe of the organized churches, or even outside them. Though it would be wrong to become obsessed with them, these latter concerns are in some ways the most intriguing religious phenomena of our times.

I hope that I shall not give offence, though I fear that I shall from time to time, which is why, in advance, I ask for indulgence and forgiveness. One or two of my journalist colleagues, on hearing of my appointment, began to treat me rather as if I had announced a sex-change operation. One, at least, said he thought I would find myself reporting the death-throes of religion in Britain. I really don't know – if so, it should at least be an enthralling story. And if I do not see it exactly your way, I hope at least you will accept my assurance of being yours – faithfully.

Crime and Punishment

22 January 1977

One of my main sources of contact with the world outside what Malcolm Muggeridge calls 'the ultimate unreality of broadcasting' is the walk I take early every morning on Hampstead Heath with my erring basset hound. During this, I meet other dog-walkers and knowing what I do for a living, they are pretty free with their comments on it. The other day they were complaining about the way reporters had gathered around the execution of Garry Gilmore – the Utah murderer – 'like a flock of vultures'. And they were still more disgusted at the prospect of a forthcoming execution in Texas being done 'live' (so to speak) on television.

I have to admit that I have many reservations of my own about the way we spend our time and money on what is rated as news, but when people go on to say 'What dreadful people those Americans are!' there are a few background points to be made on the subject of punishment.

Firstly, the people who complain about the publicity are usually very much in favour of the death penalty: I wonder if society should not know, even see, what it is ordering to be done to its criminals? Public executions, then? You would think that if the death penalty really was a deterrent, putting it on in public would deter absolutely – though I seem to remember it wasn't all that successful in the past, and there are certain other objections in these days when we worry so much about displays of violence. The next point is that those dreadful Americans are in some ways the most Christian people I know – in terms, anyway, of enthusiastic church-going and devotion to the fundamentals of the Bible. Garry Gilmore, after all, was shot in Utah, the Mormon State – and Mormons root their morality very firmly in Scripture. According to Gilmore's lawyer, Gilmore felt he should die because of the Mormon doctrine of 'blood atonement' – some sins being too terrible for even the blood of Christ to wash away. Gilmore felt his punishment was fair.

Something akin to, if not entirely identical with, this spirit, seems to be gaining ground in Britain too. Last week, in a speech that received too little attention in my view, Sir Fred Catherwood (once of National Economic Development or 'Neddy' fame) gave a roasting to what he called 'the humanist experiment in the secularization of society'. It had been assumed, he said, that having abolished God, knowledge alone would make men rational, co-operative, responsible and happy. But now the experiment was heading for the rocks, with juvenile crimes of violence multiplied seventeenfold in twenty-five years and various other signs of decay and collapse. Christians, said Sir Fred, believed that *all* men were sinners, not just the capitalists and reactionaries among us; that sin was inherent, not dependent upon environment, and that we all needed the discipline of the law. We should be prepared to tighten up our principles when necessary, for man's inhumanity to man needed some restraint.

Add to that an interesting article in the new Evangelical fortnightly *Third Way*. Written by Nick Miller, an Inner London social research officer who has also done work at Cambridge on criminology, it sums up the research of a group of experts which has been studying the law of punishment. Like C. S. Lewis, they believe that the proper reason for sentencing an offender is that quite simply he deserves his sentence. I think the word 'deserves' begs the question rather, but the article argues that in recent years the emphasis has been on reform or deterrence. This particular group wants to shift the balance away from the offender and *his* problems and back to the offence. No, they are not being cruel or vindictive, they say, but they do want the same punishment for the same crime for everyone before every court. That, they insist, is both fair and biblical.

I put it to Nick Miller, when I met him, that it might be Old Testament biblical, all right, but what about the New? He denied they were in any sense at odds, but, he added, 'I agree the New Testament says very little specifically about the penal law. We're relying largely on the first five books of the Bible.'

I must confess that kind of remark makes me feel rather shut in and glum. I suppose I might have suggested that our Lord himself did not seem terribly keen on punishment – witness, for example, the case of the woman taken in adultery, who was rescued from a fate that was then regarded as entirely biblical and fair. But the argument will, no doubt, continue. I think we shall be hearing a lot more about crime and punishment and our just desserts.

On Being a Christian

29 January 1977

This month has seen the publication here in Britain of what, by any standard, has to be called a *magnum opus*: *On Being a Christian* by the Swiss-German Roman Catholic theologian, Hans Küng. It came out first in Germany where it has sold 160,000 copies. Now Collins have brought it out in a translation by Father Edward Quinn, and for £7.95 you get 720 pages of book – which is not bad value these days, even as bulk.

But much more than bulk, you get one of the blockbusters of modern religious literature. I have heard one English scholar claim that it maps out the landscape of theology for the next fifty years. Another compares it to the masterly performance of a great symphony. A work on such a scale is bound to have some weak spots to pick at, and from a layman's point of view it has to be said that Professor Küng is rather a wordy man: he has to say everything from left to right, then right to left, then top to bottom and bottom back to top. But at least, after that, there can be no mistaking his meaning.

Like his earlier books on priesthood and infallibility, *On Being a Christian* has helped to get Professor Küng up to his neck in holy hot water – condemned by Vatican Radio, admonished by the German hierarchy, warned by the Holy Office to stop teaching error. Some Roman Catholic theologians have branded Professor Küng a Protestant. Some Protestants may think it a privilege to have him numbered among them. But in fact Rome has stopped short of excommunicating him, for he remains a priest and insists he is a loyal Catholic – in the sense (he says) that he tries to respond to people of all beliefs, including atheists, agnostics and 'seekers' of all sorts. Küng sees himself as a true ecumenist.

The sheer architecture of a book on such a scale is breathtaking yet the author does manage to hold it together. What does it mean, he asks, to be a Christian in the modern humanistic world? He does not condemn such a world, for he declares that humanism and Christianity are not opposites. Christianity cannot be properly understood, he thinks, except as radical humanism. On the flyleaf of my own copy of the book, Küng wrote for me, 'Being a true human being, by being a Christian.'

The book remarks that to many non-Christians, the Christian seems less than fully a man. It is the lack of genuine humanity, especially on the part of priests and preachers, that gets Christianity rejected. Out of sympathy, indeed in violent collision, with much of the official Roman doctrine, Küng says the one criterion of what is Christian must be Christ and the central part of the book deals penetratingly, uncompromisingly with the life and teachings of Jesus. Küng writes: 'Jesus is not interested in universal, theoretical or poetical love. It is not love of man in general, but quite concretely love of one's immediate neighbour – anyone who wants me here and now.'

Again, Küng has a splendid passage on what I would call the rat race – which he calls 'The Achievement Game'. This, he says, deceives us into thinking that success must be measured by our performance as a businessman, a scientist, a journalist, instead of quite simply as a human being. Achievements, good and bad, are not what count in the end – we must not let them dehumanize us.

But how does being a Christian help? Christians, repeats Küng, are as human as anyone else, but in the light of Jesus they can see man and his God together, and with unshakeable trust. Like Jesus, man should entrust himself to God in all things at all times, and take what God wants to give him, for God wills our welfare. Such a trust – switched on all the time and not, as most of us do, intermittently as an option – enables the Christian, unlike other humanists, to cope not only with what is beautiful, good and true, but with what is ugly, agonizing and evil. What is proclaimed here, says Küng, provides life with a solid basis, despite all the inevitable failures, and this can liberate it from the secular pressure for achievement, and bestow upon it a freedom which can sustain it even through the worst of situations. (I wish I had time here to quote that passage all over again, so profound is the comfort it has to offer.)

Altogether it is a magnificent and sustaining work. A paperback edition now follows – although I wish I could persuade Professor Küng to allow a condensed version to be made.*

*One will be published early in 1979, by William Collins.

Human Rights

5 February 1977

Among the subjects to be discussed by the General Synod of the Church of England when it meets in Westminster the week after next is human rights. That can mean a lot of things, of course, but in the present context it means, in particular, the treatment and mistreatment of Christians behind the Iron Curtain (let us not pretend no such drapery exists). The World Council of Churches took the matter up, partly to counterbalance the emphasis it appeared to be giving to black liberation movements, and is now calling on member churches to support its activities in this field, in particular the setting up of an Advisory Group on Human Rights at the Council's headquarters in Geneva.

The Church of England has had a study group under the Bishop of Kingston, Hugh Montefiore, pondering these things in a churchly sort of way – considering whether the language being used by the World Council is consonant with Christian belief, reviewing the relevant biblical material, advising what response should be made. The principal motion before the Synod will express the belief that 'The Christian understanding of man as made in the divine image places a responsibility upon the Church to support action to recognize and safeguard human rights'. A further motion calls upon the Church of England's Board for Social Responsibility to engage in what it calls 'specific activities in the field of human rights on behalf of the Church'.

Now not all members of Synod will be wild with enthusiasm about this. In the past voices have been raised complaining that human rights are a sinister humanist concern in which the Church has no business to meddle. I have even heard it said that, just as it was wrong that the Church of England should come to be thought of as the Tory Party at prayer, so it would be equally wrong for it to be thought of as Amnesty International on its knees. It should not be allowed to appear (or so goes this argument) that the Church is just one more room in the 'House of the Liberal Consensus'. What the Church *ought* to be doing is preaching the Gospel, and in answer to embarrassing cries of 'What Gospel?' we may not assume this has anything to do with trendy ideas about human rights, democracy or even society.

I do not think it would be altogether fair to call this view reactionary, though some will no doubt do so. Its proponents would, I am sure, hasten to agree that Christians should take their stand on national and international issues. It is organized religion, the Church, that is held to have no such right or duty. The Church (goes the argument) should get on with the business of fighting the moral dilapidation all around us, and leave politics to the politicians – who handle it, as we know, with sophistication and sometimes success.

Not for me to take sides in this debate. In any case, I am much too fascinated listening to everybody else. I recall, for example, the impressive and far from trendy figure of Archbishop Edward Scott, Primate of Canada, telling the World Council that nowadays it just was not possible to avoid political gestures, since even abstention was construed as a political act. I have also noted in several churches here and there, a reaction away from social and political commitment, an emphasis on what is often called spirituality, almost out of despair with the apparent futility of action, the powerlessness of the Church. 'What good does action do anyway?' is the feeling.

So back to preaching the Gospel; but the question of *what* Gospel has still to be answered. One side takes the incarnation as symbolizing God's own engagement in the everyday world. 'Thy Kingdom come – on earth' is taken by this party as a call to reformist action here and now. 'Ah,' comes the retort. 'But – "My Kingdom is not of this world".' And so the exchange of texts goes on. As a contribution to the argument, no more and no less, I find myself going back to Hans Küng's *On Being a Christian*, which I mentioned in my last talk. The Church, says Küng, may, should and must take a stand publicly, but only where the Gospel (and not just some theory of our own) demands this unambiguously.

North of the Border

12 February 1977

Getting off the train in Scotland nowadays an Englishman tends to feel a bit guilty if he doesn't instantly notice how different and 'national' it all is. Looking about me carefully in Glasgow, I noticed that the sugar-lumps in the B.B.C. canteen had been marked 'Specially wrapped for Scotland' (which is more than they do for England), and all over the walls of the city were stickers saying, 'For free information concerning the mark of the Beast, write to Stewarton Bible School, Kilmarnock.'

But the distinctive marks of Scotland go a great deal deeper than wrapping paper and stickers. Last week I was talking about that school of thought in the Church of England which maintains that religion and politics should be kept apart. A few days later I was listening to a former Moderator of the Church of Scotland declaring, 'To allow a divorce between religion and politics is a most dangerous dichotomy . . . We are very much concerned with the future of Scotland in all its aspects.' And in saying so, the former Moderator was only affirming the orthodox teaching of the Kirk as regards Church and State: the Church leads and the State follows.

In keeping with that, last year's General Assembly of the Kirk called upon every synod and presbytery to consider devolution with 'particular reference to the basic moral and spiritual factors inseparable from the political'. I attended one such gathering for Lothian, near Edinburgh, and it was both earnest and well-attended, though a great deal more political than spiritual.

It was clear from the start that the assembled ministers and elders were highly suspicious of where devolution might lead them. There was a rumble of 'hear hears' when one minister said it was not possible to talk calmly about devolution until they had determined – by a further question on the referendum – that the majority of people did *not* want devolution as a first step to separation.

The present Moderator, Professor Thomas Torrance, made a characteristically original contribution to the discussion. What shook him about the whole devolution debate (he said) was its lack of profundity: it had failed to touch the absolutism of the House of Commons, which was set towards totalitarianism. His listeners were impressed, if a trifle confused, as he went on to speak of Ireland and the House of Lords.

All this is very different from the Church of England's own synod which has not debated devolution at all, and if it had would not, I think, have laid down its line in such detail. The Scots Kirk has been voting for devolution since 1946, and thirty years later was calling for 'an effective form of self-government for Scotland, under the Crown within the framework of the United Kingdom, with adequate financial and economic powers and control of a reasonable proportion of North Sea oil revenue'. More than that, the General Assembly (which doesn't want the name 'Assembly' to be usurped by any secular newcomer) has persistently demanded that elections to any Scottish legislature should be by the single transferable vote system, and not what it calls the 'X-system'. Otherwise, it warns, the Scottish National Party could be the largest party in Scotland with only 35 per cent of the votes – just as the Labour Party has been.

At the other end of the ecclesiastical spectrum, Scotland's Roman Catholics are fearful that a new legislature might put control over education in the hands of leftists – or, almost as bad, Presbyterians – and choke off the finances of the already hard-pressed Roman Catholic schools and training colleges. One Scot in five is a Roman Catholic, and their voices have almost certainly influenced the trend shown in the opinion polls towards keeping things constitutionally as they are.

Scotland, then, really *is* different – perhaps because the Scottish Reformation was a truly Calvinist Reformation and because the Scots are a more serious people, more concerned about authority despite their dislike of hierarchy. Historically their Church Assembly has taken the place of a Parliament. Perhaps with the coming of a legislature again the Kirk will confine itself to doctrine and morality, though I doubt it. But I can't help wondering what the effect would be if the General Synod of the Church of England started passing resolutions demanding proportional representation and effective self-government for England.

Monkey Business

19 February 1977

I have been hoping to get a word in sooner or later about that religious education teacher in my native county of Hertfordshire who was suspended for propagating the literal truth of the Genesis creation story. Notice I did not say 'myth'. It makes a neat reversal of the celebrated 'Monkey Trial' in Tennessee, fifty years ago, in which John T. Scopes was found guilty by the People of advocating Darwinism. That particular law remained on the State Statutes for a long time after, and I'm not sure it isn't there still. Things don't change quickly in Tennessee.

Now, I don't want to take sides in this dispute about Adam and Eve – they may still be *sub judice*, and I don't want to be hauled up myself for contempt of anybody. But I must say, I should be very sorry to see the Bible robbed of its standing as poetry and turned into just another historical textbook. Religion, surely, is much more than literal history and we belittle our God if we try to factualize him. Religious talk is essentially poetry.

Creation stories – I will dare to say myths now – are especially poetic, the world over. Alongside the great mystery of 'Where are we going?' stands the equal mystery of 'Where did we come from?'

I am not so keen on the complex and often bloodthirsty myths of people like the Greeks, Egyptians and Babylonians: offspring devoured by their parents, gods and monsters hacked in pieces and scattered about the heavens. I like very simple myths, often beginning with an egg. The Finns have one in which the Great Sorcerer, slumbering deep in the ocean, raises one knee above the surface and upon it a passing bird lays an egg, which rolls off, shatters, and becomes the sun and moon and stars. There is a magical and neglected piece about it by the composer Sibelius.

Most sensible people give up worrying about what there was before anything was. In the beginning, they agree, there just *was* the Earth or the sea or this egg – some sort of starting point had to be. One or two myths, like that of the Iroquois, say we are the second people. The first people lived in the heavens, until one of them – a princess – fell through a hole in the sky and plopped down into the sea, where the waiting animals built an island for her.

In Mozambique there's a much simpler story still. In the beginning God dug two holes in the ground. From one he pulled out a man, from the other a woman. He gave them seed, digging sticks and a cooking pot, and told them to get on with their daily tasks. But instead they ran off into the forest to play and make love and this made God angry. He took two monkeys out of the trees, cut off their tails and stuck them on the man and the woman, saying, 'Monkeys, now you are people! People, you are the monkeys!' It explains perfectly, I think, those happy, carefree people who now swing in the trees – and us monkeys, sweating it out in the fields.

In some of the Pacific islands they tell how Old Spider found herself inside a giant clam shell, and turned the bottom half into the sea and the top half into the heavens. Old Spider, of course, brought light into the world like so many originators and heroes. But there is a pleasant Melanesian myth which sees things differently. In the beginning, it says, there was nothing but desert and perpetual light. The spirit Qat not only carved the figures of man and woman and brought them to life by dancing before them, beating his drum; when they became weary of everlasting day, Qat brought them the cooling gift of night.

A lot of these myths bear the conviction that, once upon a time, God lived among men as the Great Chief. There is a hint of the incarnation in this. Indeed, in Madagascar they say that in the beginning, God sent his son What-A-Strange-Thing to Earth but that it was too hot for him so he plunged into the cool depths of the sea and was never seen again. Since then God has continued sending his people to Earth to find What-A-Strange-Thing, but in the end each of us has to return sadly to God to report our failure. In consolation, he sends the rain.

There are so many more I wish I had time for – the Masai, the Japanese, the Zulus – but I must end with my favourite, a myth of infinite poignancy that comes from the Congo. In the beginning, it says, God lived in the Great Chief's house, and although he was never seen in the village everyone knew he was there and every day food and drink were left in gourds on the doorstep for him. One day, however, the girl whose duty it was to leave the offerings disobeyed the ancient rule. She hid behind a bush to spy upon him, and, says the story, she saw the jewelled arm of God reach out and take the gourds. He knew, of course, that he had been seen for he felt something go out of him. And that night God left the village, climbed into his canoe and paddled away down river, and has been gone from us ever since . . .

The Martyrs of Uganda

26 February 1977

A few days ago I was sitting among the archives of the Church Missionary Society, reading the story of how Christianity came to Uganda, exactly a century ago. And as I read, there was an eerie feeling of history repeating itself.

The ruler of Uganda in 1877 was the Kabaka Mtesa, a great admirer of the British. Indeed, here was one of many cases of colonization by invitation. For the archives contain a letter from the Kabaka addressed to 'My dear friend wite man', urging him to come quickly. And come the white man did, in the shape of Church of England missionaries, only to find that what the Kabaka really wanted was defence aid (to use the modern euphemism) – guns and ammunition – and that he was surrounded by Arab bodyguards and advisers who deeply resented the Christians and poisoned his ears against them. The first Anglican bishop to arrive, John Hannington, was bound and led away to a jungle butchery where he was hacked to pieces. Mtesa's heir, the Kabaka Mwanga, was even more of a monster. His hobby was debauching a corps of 500 pageboys, and when some forty Christian converts among them resisted his advances, he rolled them up in straw mats and burned them alive. They were Uganda's first martyrs, but not, it seems, its last.

Martyrdom is a strong word and some say it has yet to be established in the case of the late Archbishop Jawani Luwum of Uganda. But it was certainly being used by Kampala's Christians within a few days of the Archbishop's disappearance, and the barest, non-conjectural facts about that disappearance are enough to make the blood run cold. There is still no answer to the crucial demand, 'Show us the Archbishop's body'. In the face of such black holes in the fabric, assurances of how normal life is in Uganda and what a decent, jolly chap President Amin is remind one of those tributes to Hitler's Germany and Stalin's Russia. Both dictators, I recall, were said to be fond of children.

One has only to read the full text of the Ugandan bishops' letter – the one that speaks of 'the gun pointed at every Christian in the Church' – to sense the terror behind it: the terror and the first-century courage. Recalling the days of the Kabakas, it is only too easy to believe in that praetorian guard of foreigners around President Amin, fanning his resentment of Christians, pledging him arms and immortality. One can only wonder if their sponsors, from Tripoli to Moscow, are proud of the connection. We might, in Britain, allow ourselves some pride in having done the right thing in rescuing thousands of Ugandan Asians from such men. But it would be irresponsible to underline the situation as one of Christians against Muslims, and equally dangerous to confirm Amin's paranoid suspicions of a white conspiracy to invade his country and overthrow him.

The President of Uganda has been performing a one-man pantomime on the theme of coming to London for the Jubilee Commonwealth Conference, and there has been solemn huffing and puffing on this side about preventing him from coming. I am not sure it wouldn't be a good idea to let him come and suffer the consequent ordeal and the exposure to his peers from other Commonwealth nations. What is quite useless now, I think, is to condemn the African states for failing to condemn the tyrant. Many of them are equally insecure, almost equally guilty, and scared of Uganda's overgrown armed strength, besides being bound to silence by a convenient code of racial solidarity.

To call the African states hypocrites may be accurate, but in Africa, as elsewhere, it is a hypocritical world. That should not surprise us. Denouncing the Africans is an easy way to score righteousness points (if you enjoy the game). It may even let off justified steam, but it does nothing to help the Ugandans – any more than putting advertisements in the London papers, as has been done recently, linking the World Council of Churches with the deaths of the Jesuit missionaries in Rhodesia, does anything constructive in *that* direction, either. But then, martyrs by definition are not there to object.

In a sense, the fact that these disasters occur at all means that it is already too late – that we have long ago failed to understand what is going on and to make peace happen. Nevertheless, the murdered Jesuits, Bishop Lamont convicted of aiding terrorists, and Archbishop Luwum himself – different though their circumstances may have been – all did what they felt they had to do in the face of irresistible armed force. Or rather, they were what they had to be, even if that was construed as interfering in politics. All of them met the crisis with prayer. All of them, as Christians, must have shared the belief of Martin Luther King in the redemptive power of unmerited suffering. Yet here we are again, debating how to tidy things up by deposing President Amin. Maybe we have missed the point. Maybe we are looking for the wrong lesson in all this.

Black Islam

12 March 1977

I hope those who expect a purely Christian homily will forgive an attempt to say something this morning about the so-called Hanafi Black Muslims, whose violence in seizing an office building in Washington has shocked black and white, Christian and Muslim alike.

The group presumably claim to be a connection of that sub-branch of the Shia Muslims which gave the British Empire so much trouble with a succession of Mad Mullahs and Mahdis. But in fact they are a splinter group of the Negro 'Nation of Islam', which in origin had very little to do with the Prophet or the holy Koran. It must all be somewhat embarrassing to the true Islamic states of the Middle East, whose very success in beating the white man at the oil game helped to lend Islam so much prestige in the eyes of American blacks. Yet it goes back much further than that.

America's emancipated slaves had been made to feel that their African origins were something primitive and shameful. Some of them looked for an ideology that was non-white, yet not black, but militant and successful. Vaguely they heard of the Arabs and Islam.

During the First World War, thousands of Negroes moved up to the factories of Detroit and Chicago, away from the framework of their compliant southern churches and into competition with equally poor whites. Race rioting broke out, dozens were killed, and the hypocrisy of white Christianity was supposedly unmasked.

Not many blacks took the Muslim road at first. Perhaps the earliest was Timothy Drew, or 'Noble Drew Ali', who wore a fez and founded 'Temples of Moorish Science', at least one of which still existed in Chicago a few years ago. Next on the scene was Wallace Ford – alias 'Wali Farrad' – half-Jamaican, half-Syrian, a pedlar of cheap raincoats who claimed to have come from Mecca. His speciality was selling people what he claimed were their original pre-slave names, which – oddly, in view of the Arab role in the slave trade – turned out to be pseudo-Muslim.

Farrad, Ford or Fard got into trouble with the police over a peculiarly nasty murder which was rumoured to have been a human sacrifice. He may, in the end, have been sacrificed himself, because he vanished entirely – some say into the depths of Lake Michigan, wearing a concrete shroud – and was replaced by his disciple Elijah Poole, son of a Southern Baptist minister.

Elijah Muhammad, as he was now called, was a typical southern-style preacher who proceeded to devise a diabolical theology of his own. Man, said Elijah, had originally been black but 6,645 years ago an evil scientist called Yakub (probably based upon the Jacob of Jacob and Esau) had cheated the black man of his rights. By employing selective birth control, he had produced a degenerate race of white, blue-eyed devils, who ever since had sought to pollute the black race with their filthy seed. It is an extremely violent and racist doctrine but in practical terms Elijah advocated separation. Ultimately an all-black State was to be carved out of the American south, but for the time being a lucrative black business empire selling ritual robes and foodstuffs to the faithful was set up. At the last estimate it was said to be worth some £25,000,000 ($50,000,000). Under Elijah's uncouth leadership the Black Muslims nevertheless became prosperous, bourgeois, worldly. With Elijah's death in 1975 his son Wallace succeeded non-violently to the leadership and has since been phasing out the racism, I am glad to say.

But there have always been puritanical breakaway groups. The most notable was one headed by Malcolm X, once a vicious criminal who was actually transformed by making the pilgrimage to Mecca and learning something of the true Islam. Malcolm was gunned down in his own New York temple for criticizing Elijah's morals – in much the same way as the Hanafi women and children were slaughtered in Washington some years later. The Hanafi group regarded Elijah's movement as heretical and evidently they wanted to make boxer Muhammad Ali (one of Elijah's star converts) recant. One of the things they suppose to be justified by Islam is anti-Semitism, though I am inclined to trace this back to a long-standing Negro dislike of Jewish shopkeepers, often accused of exploiting the black ghettos.

It is important, I think, to exonerate the true Islam from any responsibility for all this: indeed, the Islamic ambassadors who were called in as mediators at the Washington siege did play an important part in averting a worse tragedy. It may be that the presence in Britain of an authentic Muslim community from Pakistan will discourage any obscene parodies of the faith from taking root here. Rastafarianism – a West Indian cult of the late Emperor Haile Selassie of Ethiopia – may be taking that place. Perhaps we should still wonder how it was that the Christian churches in America lost the poor blacks, and whether the churches here may not be losing them, too.

A Larger Constituency

19 March 1977

Over the past few weeks I have been to no fewer than four different conferences on religious broadcasting. Goodness knows, the conference industry seems to flourish almost regardless of what is being conferred about, and no branch of the communications business is more interested in pulling itself up and examining its own roots and flowers than Religion.

But before we get carried away, do we know who listens to religious broadcasts anyway – if anybody? According to my statistical sources, three-quarters of you are women, almost the same proportion is over fifty, less than one in ten under thirty: hardly a cross-section of the population. From this various deductions could be drawn, among them, that religious broadcasting should concentrate on the elderly – or that it had better start learning a completely different language if it hopes to have any audience at all in the future. I hope, personally, that it is allowed to combine both approaches.

In the course of my conferring I did hear some voices sternly declare, 'Leave society alone: your job is to preach the Gospel – or what *I* mean by the Gospel!' More churchmen than I expected were prepared to say, as one Jesuit did, 'When we use words like sacrament and atonement these days we might as well be speaking Chinese to most people.' Another contributor – a noted television producer – said, 'I don't think the Church realizes how totally it has lost credibility with the rising generation. It's more of a hindrance to us than a help in trying to broadcast the Gospel. When I started my most successful series,' added this producer, 'I had to ban clergymen from appearing on it, in the interests of making it credible.' The clergy present did not contest that statement. It was one of the bishops among them who remarked, 'The obligations of broadcasting are to a larger constituency than the churches.'

Which leads me to the point, unpalatable to some I know, that what I and my colleagues are officially engaged in nowadays is officially described as *religious* broadcasting, not *Church* broadcasting. What I understand by that is not just that we have to bear in mind other faiths like Judaism and Islam, but that we must also speak to the condition of people who are outside the traditional forms of faith but by no means indifferent to a religious interpretation of life. There is a controversial choice here, as I can see: whether to 'go with them' and listen with sympathy to what these spiritual free-lances are trying to say, or whether to try to shepherd them back into the fold, tut-tutting about humanism and trendiness as we do so. I know which I think adds to life, rather than subtracts from it.

Two other points of discussion stick in my mind. The first is the problem of Christian comment on matters of topical controversy. My own feeling as a journalist is that there is usually far too much comment nowadays and not enough finding out what actually happened in the first place. In any case, I am inclined to agree that there is no such exclusive commodity as Christian comment, though there is comment by Christians. Even so, I fancy there may be a sort of higher objectivity, based upon the universal fatherhood of God, which should make the Christian rather a bad Party man, reluctant to jump aboard the bandwagon and dismiss any of his fellow men as mere Communists or Fascists, terrorists or policemen. Loving one another has to involve listening to one another, and taking seriously things that we would rather not hear.

Yet the other point is this: the whole doctrine of objectivity in public service broadcasting can become a terrible strait-jacket when you are trying to present prophets and visionaries, trying to break through to a new language and new symbols which are alive today. How could one possibly 'balance' the prophet Isaiah, or, indeed, the Sermon on the Mount? Broadcasting has always found the controversial hard to handle. Yet orthodoxy has never been the test of the true prophet. To quote my colleague again: 'Perhaps we play too safe, perhaps we don't claim enough for the media.' Why can't the television programme itself become a sacrament, an icon, a moment of religious communion? Why shouldn't broadcasting be able to express the sublime heights of faith, just as the windows of Chartres did in their day? And does it have to be called *religious* broadcasting? I recall the words of that profoundly religious non-churchman, the playwright Dennis Potter: 'To write for the God-slot would be to abdicate my responsibility.'

Mother India

26 March 1977

Some years ago I was sitting out under the stars in the middle of a north Indian village, digesting an excellent meal of *matta-paneer* (or cheese and peas) and listening to the gossip round an open fire. Or rather, a friend who spoke the local Hariana dialect was giving me a running translation. One old fellow, the oldest inhabitant, was saying, 'I remember when Muhammad of Ghazni was here, and then when the Moguls came. After that it was the British, now it's the Congress, and next it will be the Communists. It all depends on who's got the biggest stick and who grabs whose buffalo first . . .'

Nobody challenged his memory of several centuries of history or the wisdom distilled from it, but in fact the recent Indian elections which threw out Mrs Indira Gandhi and installed the Janata Party suggest that the Indian voter is much less inclined to lie back and allow himself to be walked over than he (and she) used to be. I am not saying whether the change of Government is going to make everybody better off or not, but the rather patronizing assumption that only the pinko-greys know which end of a ballot-box is which seems destined for the scrap heap.

As indeed are a lot of other assumptions that church

people, and people in general, tend to make about the extraordinary country that is India. I myself have been as guilty as anybody. Sitting out on yet another starlit night in Delhi, I was holding forth about the duty of Christian missionaries to spread the faith among the heathen Hindu. An Indian gentleman beside me gently begged to differ and said that if God had chosen to make a man a Hindu he thought it blasphemy to tinker with God's choice. 'But I as a Christian, must insist . . .' I said. 'I too am a Christian,' he responded. 'Ah, but if it had not been for the British missionaries you could not have been,' I insisted. 'On the contrary,' he told me. 'You see, I am from Malabar: our church was founded directly by St Thomas in A.D. 52. We never proselytize and we get on extremely well with our neighbours the Hindus and Muslims, and the black and white Jews of Cochin. Perhaps you didn't know about them either.'

I stood reproved. Ever since then I have insisted, wherever I could, that for all her upheavals, India deserves a great deal of respect for her toleration of religious variety. At the same time, the Churches of North and South India have set Christians everywhere an example of how to achieve unity. Occasionally there are outbreaks of drastic intolerance – there can be no doubt that fundamentally India sees herself as a Hindu nation, even *the* Hindu nation. But for a nation that also has as many Muslims as there are in the whole of Pakistan, and more Christians than there are in Portugal, things go remarkably smoothly. I don't think we give India credit for running as well as she does. Like her own incredible railway system, she may not be very fast, modern or luxurious, but she gets there in the end, in spite of all our snooty predictions of disaster.

Since I first went to work there more than twenty years ago, India's population has come within sight of doubling itself, at 620,000,000. Small wonder that the authorities have been tempted to some rather drastic measures of birth control to keep it down. As the Archbishop of Canterbury, Dr Donald Coggan, remarked: 'It is hardly the sort of country where you would feel called to preach on the text, "Be fruitful and multiply".' But the miracle is that somehow India has managed to feed her enormous population, that there have not been (as there were in the last days of British rule) mass deaths from starvation. And if you think I am callously glossing over the facts of abject misery and malnutrition, then I must direct you to another Indian miracle which I think should give Western Christians cause for reflection and thanksgiving.

Once you have got over the initial panic of living among so many millions of people in a country so utterly unlike England, the visitor to India can discover that it is very far from being a land of despair. Deplorable though institutions like the caste system and untouchability may be to us, Hinduism does confer upon these millions a stability, security, at times even colour and joy without which their lives really would be intolerable. Christianity has a fine and admired record of bringing India health, education and an example of voluntary charitable service. But I must say that it was the ordinary Hindu in the village who compelled me to grasp the meaning of 'Blessed are the poor in spirit – Blessed are the meek'.

Violence and Political Change

2 April 1977

Recently at King's College, London, there was a remarkable lecture given on the subject of 'Violence and Political Change', with particular reference to Northern Ireland. The Professor of Moral Theology at Maynooth, the Reverend Enda McDonagh, was calling upon the Irish churches to get into the Ulster political situation and, by non-violent struggle, take it over from the men of violence.

The violence of the gunmen, he thinks, is inhuman, barbaric, simply impossible to justify. But it is not enough to denounce them – which is good to hear in an age when challenging people to denounce things has become an easy way of bypassing what really matters. Father McDonagh goes on: 'I can identify with men of violence to some degree because of my historical background and because I know the thrust of violence in myself . . . That understanding leads me to sympathize with some of their frustrations and to share some of their goals.' Well, there speaks an honest man, and Father McDonagh builds upon this to insist that outsiders who are not committed to the struggle have no right to offer doctrinaire advice about violence.

One of the few points on which I personally part company with the Professor is his acceptance of the fashionable idea that violence can be attributed to institutions as well as to people. I know that in Ireland 'institutional violence' is a code word meaning 'the British Army', but it still seems to me a kind of pathetic fallacy (in the true sense of that term) which can be used to justify counter-violence where none is really justifiable. Violence is committed by responsible individuals, not by abstractions. However, it is certainly true that non-violence is scarcely encouraged by the refusal of people to modify institutions which are not appropriate, and it is that sort of refusal which forces the concerned to join the struggle against such institutions.

Yet, says Father McDonagh, time introduces a terrible dilemma. For people at the bottom of the heap, with only one life to lead, gradual reform can mean a death sentence. The attempt to compress time by using violence sacrifices one group of victims in the present for the sake of generations yet to come. However, Father McDonagh thinks it is impossible (by use of some moral calculation) to rule out the choice of violent means for *all* times and places. One is always choosing for a *particular* time and place – and even there some people may choose violence, others non-violence, and both be making a morally good decision. There may, thinks the Professor, be deeper realities involved than purely moral ones. (One wonders here what he can mean. Not, one hopes, racial or national or historic realities.)

But there is no doubt in my mind that Father McDonagh

does personally choose non-violence. It has two great advantages, he thinks. First, as Gandhi saw, it liberates the oppressor as well as the oppressed; and second, its very use helps to exorcize society of the demons of violence, rather than rehabilitate them under some new management. McDonagh then comes to the point of action. Christian churches, people and theologians should consider opting for non-violence, not in the prayer-meeting or lecture hall, but in real engagement with the struggle for peace and justice and freedom. Such a choice will involve commitment to social and political goals – no fence-sitting – and it will involve practical training in non-violence. As Martin Luther King knew, training is just as vital to a non-violent campaign as it is to a military one. Where the decision to act has been taken, effective moral leadership is once more possible – as it is not in mere debate. Otherwise the churches are condemned to repeating wearily their denunciations of violence, with no alternative to offer.

Professor McDonagh considers that there is a long tradition of violence between England and Ireland which 'without being unduly pessimistic' could drag on into the twenty-first century. At its root is the fear that each community has of being absorbed by the other. But as Christians must know, it is love that drives out fear, and that love must extend even to the men of violence – to understanding them, restraining them and ultimately converting them. This will be achieved not by denunciation, but by commitment to rectify injustice, and by radically converting ourselves. Enda McDonagh concludes: 'To ensure a new community in Northern Ireland, a new mankind and a new Christianity may have to come to birth in both Ireland and England.'

Yes, that's what he said: '. . . and England'.

De Profundis

9 April 1977 (Holy Saturday)

I suppose that today must be the darkest moment of the Christian year: disaster has struck our Lord, injustice has done its worst, hope is extinguished in the blackness of the tomb. But we should know better than the disciples of long ago, and I have been trying to apply what we know to the kind of disaster that can strike any of us today. What I have in mind as I write is the aircraft collision on the ground at Tenerife, with its sudden obliteration of some 570 lives at one blow.

The last thing I could do, here in front of this microphone, is to attempt to offer sympathy and comfort to those who have been bereaved. In my experience, the best one can do at such a time is to be a good listener – not an unctuous talker. So far as funeral ceremonies go, I personally am more attracted to the kind that give thanks for the life of So-and-so rather than mourning their death, although this is not to say we ought to suppress our grief when it is genuine. When Dylan Thomas urged his dying father to 'Rage, rage against the dying of the light', it was Dylan himself that was raging – and healthily. If ever there was a time for people to relax the stiff upper lip, it is at a time of death.

But I am trying to speak now not to those who mourn but rather to those who ponder tragedy at a distance. What I am going to say may not be very popular, but I think it has to be said, from a Christian point of view.

For a start, I am not too happy about the way we always talk about 'innocent' victims. I am not subscribing to the view that 'we are all guilty' – even though I don't in fact believe we are always as innocent as we protest. We do too little to head off disaster. We gamble with our own lives. What I am really questioning is the assumption behind the word 'innocent' – that we are actually entitled not to die – or at least that we should be granted a length of life and style of death appropriate to what we regard as our virtues. But Christians should know that God does not preside over a heavenly Old Bailey, handing out long life and easy death to the innocent, and short lives and excruciating torment to the wicked. Christ's own passion must tell us that life is not extended as a reward for godliness.

At which point the unbeliever can say: it all goes to show that there is, in fact, no God; that life is a series of brutal accidents, most of them caused by our own folly. As usual, matters are not so simple for the believer: he has various choices before him. He can take a sternly medieval view, that the best of us are so sinful it is a wonder that God does not wipe us all out like Sodom and Gomorrah. Or he can seek comfort in the belief that we all get our true desserts in another world, as did our Lord himself. Or, like so many of us, the believer can continue to grapple with the problems of suffering, trustful that there is an answer, but accepting too that only God knows what it is. (To expect to be able to understand all God's ways is to postulate a pretty puny God – one who can think on no higher a level than our own.)

But whatever line they follow, it seems to me that Christians must all accept the following: that they must be ready to die at any moment. It is, indeed, our duty to have our souls composed for that, for no matter how virtuous or prayerful we may be, we do not know the day or the hour when our souls shall be required of us. I think we should be reminded of that rather more often from the pulpit.

I do not think this should be a cause of depression or terror, but of deep tranquillity and trust. It may sound odd to say this, but we do not have to worry about how and when we shall die. That is all being taken care of for us – and so are those we shall leave behind. And, paradoxically, a soul prepared for death is also one perfectly fitted for life as well. The most serene and happy people are often those who say, 'I've had a good life; I hope to go on having a good life; but whenever my time is up, I'm ready.' And on the other side, those least fit to die are those who cannot stand life any more. There is a good deal to be said for a sudden 'unmerited' end. Perhaps, though, I should hesitate over 'unmerited' as I did over 'innocent'. The point is, we are all under suspended sentence of death from the moment of our conception, and every day of life is a privilege extended to us by grace.

The Theology of the Motor Car

15 April 1977

The other day I was rung up by one of those magazine writers who compile articles by telephoning well-known human beings and asking them their favourite cure for hiccups or how they spent their honeymoon. This one wanted to know what I thought about my car. This started me thinking whether – as there seems to be a theology of everything else nowadays, from liberation and negritude to broadcasting and Third World development – there might not be a theology of the motor car.

Personally I have the same sort of warily neutral feeling towards my car that I have towards my shoes or my hair-brush. I don't love it and I have not given it a Christian name. I don't regard it as a work of the Devil, but neither is it one of God's creatures as far as I am concerned.

All I ask is a simple, reliable means of transport. It can take five minutes getting from nought to sixty and sixty can be its top speed provided it gets me from A to B without going wrong. Reliability is the prime virtue, not its capacity for expressing my personality, venting my frustrations at the office, or impressing the opposite sex. Naturally I think people who drive smarter, faster cars than mine, or who dare to overtake me when I am doing a nice cosy fifty-five miles an hour, are a bunch of low-grade show-offs who have to do that to compensate for their inadequacies elsewhere. But I am far too Christian to be jealous of them – instead, I pity them.

Here at once is what seems to me the main moral significance of the motor car. Either way – me being pseudo-humble and charitable, or them wallowing in extravagance and pride – the car brings out the worst in us: I suggest because it serves as a mask, a disguise, a suit of armour, making us feel we can get away with doing things we would never dream of doing on foot. Do we think that even God cannot see us through the windscreen? We and our fellow drivers cease to be ordinary human beings. People in cars we disapprove of are no longer our brothers and sisters, but competitors, enemies – even, in the case of motorless pedestrians, a lower breed of animals altogether – all of which is appallingly sinful.

So is the car itself sinful? Is it, after all, a work of the Devil? It is certainly the great Sabbath-breaker, not only in making our intended day of rest a day of restlessness, of wrestling with traffic, but also in helping us to cram into a five-day week more than human nature was ever intended to do in six – which is surely just as sacrilegious.

On further contemplation, I'm inclined to think that the car may be a sort of cross that every motorist chooses to bear. It represents the modern, technological, labour-saving life that gives us so many advantages and so much suffering. More than any other material object, it sums up the whole materialist dilemma: if you get a car you have independence, mobility, speed and all the stress, expense and danger that go with them. If you get rid of your car and return to foot and hoof you save money, have less to worry about, live the simple life – and become a sort of social misfit in the eyes of your fellows and employers.

There is, of course, the ecological argument, now given theological respectability, urging us to stop wasting a million years of God's resources on a hundred years of mechanical greed. There is also the argument that as the nation's chief violator of the commandment 'Thou shalt not kill', the car is something that every devout Christian should refuse to handle. But there seems to be a tacitly agreed blood-price for the convenience of motoring.

Frankly there isn't a hope of the churches agreeing that cars are unchristian. Too many vicars rely on them, and anyway the church is an expression of the sort of people we are – not (I'm afraid) a magical system for transforming us into what we ought to be. I don't actually think God himself is very interested in cars – he has much cleverer inventions of his own, like seagulls, rabbits and mackerel. But we are told he is intensely interested in how we treat one another – love one another, in fact – and we seem to find it extremely difficult to do that when each of us is wrapped up in a motor car. Once, in California, I saw a car with a Zen sticker on its rear bumper reading I AM ALSO A YOU which is very profound if you think about it. The problem is, how to get one Christian to see the other Christian – or Muslim, Sikh or Zoroastrian – in the car ahead.

Evangelicals

23 April 1977

Last Monday there ended at Nottingham University the second National Evangelical Anglican Congress – the first having been at Keele, ten years ago. This one ended, if with no very unified sense of direction, at least with an air of confidence and authority. In an earlier report elsewhere I said it had bitten off more than it could chew. Well, eventually – thanks to a wide-open system of participation, the like of which I have never seen anywhere before – it did chew up an enormous amount of material, though it is going to take a series of paperbacks in the months ahead to get it all digested. Perhaps the most valuable thing I can do now is to pick out some of the key points from the collection of statements issued by the various specialist groups.

As one might expect, the Congress repeatedly emphasized its faith in Jesus Christ as Lord, as God, as only Saviour of the world 'through his death in our place' – although one document registered some differences of emphasis among members regarding the atonement. It also reaffirmed the Evangelical belief in the divine inspiration of Scripture, its entire trustworthiness, the sufficiency of its teaching for salvation, and its unique authority. John Stott of All Souls, Langham Place – still the tireless sea-captain of Anglican Evangelicals – went so far as to say: 'We believe God has spoken finally in Jesus Christ – that Scripture is precisely the written speech of God' – and it's hard to get much more fundamental than that. Mr Stott, especially, resisted any charismatic notions that there could be living prophets today, with the same authority as those of the biblical age. There were, however, expressions of brotherhood towards Anglican charismatics. Incidentally, Evangelicals seem to feel they now have almost enough Bible scholars and are short of moral philosophers and systematic theologians.

The Congress still wistfully hoped for some kind of Mission to the Nation, but it accepted the view of Dr Coggan that regional enterprise is better than a huge centrally imposed campaign that might flop and do more harm than good.

There is a tradition among Evangelicals against clerical élitism – two or three groups in their statements called for bishops to have less administrative work and smaller diocesan areas. One said daringly, 'We do not think the episcopacy is essential for the existence of the Church.' But any notion of an Evangelical secession was rejected, after a couple of swipes at what were described as 'the low levels of godliness' and the 'tacit triumphalism' of the Established Church.

The Evangelicals say that in general they like Series 3, with its opportunities for experiments in colour, music and drama (of which there were some examples at Nottingham that made High Church ritual look almost dowdy). One group must have gratified the Baptists by saying, 'We accept adult baptism as the theological norm', and by going on to speak of 'safeguarding the font as we safeguard the Lord's Table'. Indiscriminate baptism and the admission of toddlers to Communion were frowned upon, as were abortion and homosexual intercourse. Parenthood was encouraged – within wedlock, one assumes.

A group dealing with ministry disapproved of one-man

parishes and wanted a shared leadership of lay presbyters. Stipendiary ministers, it said, should have at least two or three years in secular employment before they even start training. A section on the Roman Catholic Church expressed penitence for past attitudes – but came back to a series of embarrassingly loaded questions about Catholic doctrine.

A fascinating report on 'Power in Democracy' called on the Church to devote more time and money to what it called 'in-depth political education'. And a minority report in the same group insisted upon the biblical mandate for private property ownership.

One of the most fought-over sections was one dealing with the media. Thanks largely to the lobbying of young Evangelicals working in communications, its report emerged with some glowing tributes to the media and a call to the churches to support religious broadcasting, especially in local radio. (There was a fairly obvious slap here at Lord Annan and his report.)

Yet amid all the penitence and good will expressed towards the Roman Catholics, the charismatics and the Free Churches, one missed any comparable charity towards other Anglicans, especially the liberals and radicals. But to allow John Stott the final Evangelical 'thump': 'We have no cause to regret our very strong disagreement with *them*.'

Experience of Something Other

30 April 1977

The other day, in the course of a visit to Nottingham University, I stumbled upon a line of research which seems to me of profound, and in certain hands even sensational, significance to the study of religion. Precisely what that significance really is, I am still not entirely sure. There is still much work to be done in the field and at the desk, and the interpretation of it could yield in opposite directions. But I had better outline what is there so far.

Between a third and a half of the adult population of the United Kingdom seems to have had some form of direct, personal, religious experience – experience of a sort that has made them aware of a presence or power – whether or not they call it God – which is different from their everyday selves.

I have used there the definition of 'religious experience' devised by Sir Alister Hardy of Oxford and applied by Mr David Hay, lecturer in the Department of Education at Nottingham, in a series of opinion surveys taken nationally and in the Nottingham area. Working with David Hay is his associate Ann Morisey, and they have been largely financed by the Religious Experience Unit at Manchester College, Oxford.

Their discovery, particularly surprising for a country recently assessed as 'the second least religious country on earth, after Japan', can be seen as a development of work done in the United States over the past ten or twelve years. It had long been assumed that religious experience was very rare, and perhaps becoming rarer in this age of sophistication, but apparently that is far from being the case. Some figures even suggest that religious experience is on the increase. A return of the Holy Spirit? Probably not as spectacular as that. It is much more likely that survey techniques are improving and that people are becoming much less shy – since Kinsey and All That – about answering intimate questions. David Hay tells me that, time and again, people tell him of their experience and then add, 'I've never told anyone about this before – not even my husband (or wife)'. Sometimes they are afraid of ridicule; sometimes it is just too private.

But what *are* these experiences? Very few involve visions or voices. As St Teresa knew, the most authentic experiences are those which do not depend upon sensory perceptions. Mostly they are quite spontaneous, out of the blue. Somebody may be walking along the street (says David Hay) when 'Snap! Some kind of awareness of the presence of God turns up!' Small wonder they find it hard to express.

Not only does this research explode the assumption that religious experience is now rare; it also undermines several other myths. For example, that such experience is a symptom of battiness – or, to be more scientific, of neurosis or even psychosis. Again, the preliminary results of the Hay-Morisey work suggest that religious experience is associated with an unusually *high* level of psychological well-being and humane concern for the world. The Marxist view of religion as the opiate of the poor and the oppressed is similarly demolished for religious experience becomes more common the higher one moves up the social, economic and educational scale. Overall, people reporting religious experience are likely to be more stable and mentally balanced, not so likely to be poor, equally likely to be male or female, and quite commonly to have no formal link with any church. The highest positive response seems to be among people who are deeply interested or deeply committed to Christianity but cannot stomach its institutions. David Hay adds: 'It seems to me there is a sort of secret religiosity in the nation – something natural about religiousness in man – a biological awareness out of which man constructs his religion.'

This is not quite the same, it seems to me, as saying that it *is* religion. An atheist like Marghanita Laski would recognize it as the ecstasy she has been writing about for years. A Quaker might recognize it as his old friend, the light within. Such experiences are fascinating as a re-emphasis of the role of personal experience in faith, but quite a different matter from accepting Jesus as Lord, or the authority of the Holy Catholic Church. But it may be a step towards science joining, rather than knocking down, religion.

Canterbury Trails

7 May 1977

When I say that the congregation of the English Church in Geneva puts on one of the best old-fashioned evensongs in the business, and that the Domestic Chaplain to the Archbishop of Canterbury nearly blew the roof off Geneva Cathedral with his improvisations upon its stainless steel organ, I am just trying to purge my mind of its last snapshots and get down to the inner meanings of Dr Coggan's recent mission to Istanbul and back. What was it all about?

The visit showed, for one thing, that the Archbishop does not intend to let the grass grow under his feet during what will have been a relatively short term of office by the time he retires. As his travels to India and Australasia this year have shown, he is very conscious of being at the head of not just the Church of England, but the worldwide Anglican Communion. He has been to India, he is going to Russia – and what is just as important, he is newly back from Rome and Geneva.

Geneva is the headquarters of the World Council of Churches, where the churches of the Third World in particular have their meeting-place, and where there is a certain tendency to regard the Church of England as insular, miserly, patronizing and rather a drag on other, more go-ahead Anglicans. At the World Council centre, Dr Coggan was careful to present himself as one who had come to 'look, learn and listen', not to lecture. Of the Pope, the Ecumenical Patriarch and the General Secretary of the World Council, it was the latter (the West Indian Dr Philip Potter) who needed the most delicate handling. It remains to be seen now if confidence *has* been established, if Canterbury will now join the world movement in spirit as well as letter. I have my doubts.

The visit to Constantinople (if the Turks will excuse my

calling it that temporarily) was probably the most positive success. Talks with the Orthodox were on the verge of being called off because of the ordination of women priests by some branches of the Anglican Communion. Archbishop and Patriarch confronted each other across the aisle and firmly stated their positions – and then agreed not to break off their contacts, but indeed to continue and intensify them and to tackle the problem – one that greatly concerns Dr Coggan – of how to get theological agreements down from the expert committees to the grass roots of the local clergy and their people.

I suspect that Dr Coggan himself would prefer me to spotlight his call for united Christian effort in evangelizing the world, as the main theme of his trip. But I must say that what I found most intriguing was the steady development, in the Archbishop's thinking aloud, of the theme that the Holy Spirit did not cease speaking to man when the last full stop was put to the New Testament and the Creeds – that the Spirit might yet have new things to say to us, and that the ordination of women as priests (which is not an obvious biblical commandment) might be an example. Daring for an Evangelical – shocking, perhaps, to a Fundamentalist: and in this instance, both Pope and Patriarch must be counted as Fundamentalists, as are many Anglicans. Once you start quoting the Holy Spirit as your authority for innovation, there's no knowing where it may stop. At which you may cry, 'Let's hope it never will' or 'Things have gone far enough', according to taste.

But the Archbishop insists that chaos is the last thing he wants in the churches, which is the very reason he virtually paint-sprayed on the Pope's wall the slogan 'Get with what's happening – legalize intercommunion'. It didn't impress the Vatican (which thought it all rather vulgar), but then I doubt if Dr Coggan really expected much from an ageing Pope and his surprisingly unreformed Curia. Rome does not seem to be very well informed about what is going on among some of the younger English Roman Catholics: for example, the influential young priest who told me he *did* take Communion from an Anglican, *did* regard Anglican orders as valid and (in his own words) was 'trying hard to catch up with the Reformation'.

The joint statement signed by Pope and Archbishop was actually a good deal more specific and committal than has been recognized. I venture to suggest that the real future of Anglican-Roman unity depends upon local congregations reading the statement, pushing it, and insisting on its being carried through. Dr Coggan wants to proceed in decent order, he says, but whether the Holy Spirit is so orderly, we shall see.

Filthy Lucre

21 May 1977

For months since the fall of President Nixon, journalists have been trying to unearth a British Watergate – though we have never been able to match the majestic squalor of the original. Now, it seems, we are endeavouring to reconstruct a home-grown version of the Lockheed Aircraft 'Business by Bribery' scandal.

What's the religious angle on that? You might assume it is essentially the moral angle – that the churches are entitled to preach about it because corruption is wrong and religion is supposed to help keep us on the straight and narrow path of virtue. Our own, British-type path, of course.

Well, yes – but. There is actually a great deal more to religion than ethics. I will suggest in a minute that moral judgement isn't always that simple, even when you are equipped with the Ten Commandments and the Sermon on the Mount. But people seem to arrive at much the same basic code of decency whether they are Christians or not, believers or not. Religion, it seems to me, has to do with – or has also to do with – matters that go far beyond right or wrong. It has to do with why we are here at all, where we are going, and how to cope with the mess we get into when, relentlessly, we fail to do what we know, in theory, we ought to do. It should be pretty obvious by now that, Church or no Church, we are going to go on being brutal, selfish and corrupt – in which case, it takes a good religion to stop one despairing and either turning brigand oneself, or ending it all.

I said moral judgement is not that simple. I believe I heard the Christian businessman Sir Fred Catherwood arguing on the air the other morning that while it was clearly wrong to employ bribes to make a Government buy aircraft X rather than aircraft Y, there were many situations in the world today where you had to regard a certain amount under the counter as part of your business expenses – a kind of unofficial tax or facilities fee. In fact, this is a system that works quite well, though the British have a reputation abroad of being rather miserly with the slush compared with the Japanese and French. I suspect that the Arab or African who accepts the money would feel insulted at hearing it called a bribe. Not to offer it would be to class his services as worthless, to belittle him. So is it fair to blame the man who gives the bribe?

A couple of weeks ago I was in Istanbul, where a riot had just taken place and thirty-four people had been shot dead in the square. I wanted to get the story to London – not just to make the British gasp, but to inform listeners to the Turkish Service of the B.B.C. about what was really going on in their country. But when I approached the hotel telephone operator to put through the call, she made a great show of flashing lights and snapping switches and vowed she could not possibly manage it. I remembered that she was still unrewarded after my last telephone call, so I wrote the London number on a piece of paper, folded a Turkish £5 note underneath it and slid it across the counter to her. She got the message and so did the B.B.C. in London.

Now, who was corrupting whom? My job is to get the news back – legally, of course – and although I am not actually encouraged to write 'Bribe to Turkish telephone operator – £5' on my account sheet, the B.B.C. will eventually reimburse me, one way or another. Which hints at more corruption, perhaps – the notorious swindle-sheet, or expense account, of the honest British journalist. Another aspect of the current rumpus is the curious effect of *scale* on our moral values. We quietly pillage our workplaces, taking home stationery, review copies, offcuts and seconds of this and that, but huff with outrage when a big corporation gets caught doing something equally normal – equally illegal. And if *Government* gets caught, it's carnival time!

I haven't any kind of unconditional verdict on this and I am not condemning anybody. The main purpose of condemnation seems to be to dissociate the commentator from the crime and emphasize his own righteousness. No, I do not think we should turn a blind eye to outrageous corruption. There are limits to everything. But I do think we should be slow to brand the man who gets caught as if he were a monster of depravity quite unlike ourselves – which reminds me that depravity is a distinct theological term for the innate corruption of man – a condition calling for understanding, love and mercy.

Edinburgh Rock

28 May 1977

On the eve of the General Assembly of the Church of Scotland, which I have been attending this week, I wandered into its rather dingy Gothic palace up on Edinburgh's rock. The corridors smelt strongly of carbolic (like the Vatican, incidentally), as if being sterilized of sin. But there was already a pile of crisp handouts in the press-room. Some passages in one caught my eye. If, it said, so many parishes had not been merged, and if all the churches had been retained with a minister for each, the Kirk would now be short of something like 1,500 ministers. Or, if it actually had them, it would be paying out a further £3,500,000 ($7,000,000) which it hadn't got. 'At the last General Assembly,' said the handout, 'we were accused of defeatism and lack of faith. But where is the line between faith and blind credulity? Does faith mean ploughing blindly on in the same old rut, without learning any lessons whatsoever from our past experience?' At this point I noticed the date at the top of the handout: it was 24 May 1976. The paper had been sitting there foı the past year.

But the handout was no less relevant for that. The most pressing reports to come before this year's Assembly had a very similar story to tell and much the same warning to utter. The Church of Scotland will need, for 1978, a total income of almost £18,000,000. That is, £3,000,000 more than this year. But if the Kirk continues to lose members at the present, well-established rate, there will be 20,000 fewer members to raise it. The majority of church members, we are told, put 35p or less into the plate each week. Indeed, if you deduct the Kirk's investment income, it looks as if they are giving something nearer 27p. (Let me hasten to add, I am not suggesting that English churchgoers are necessarily more generous.)

The figures are bad all round. Fewer ministers, fewer elders, congregations, communicants – and the communicants are communicating less often. Donations are increasing, in fact, but through inflation are falling more and more behind the budget. Drastic cutbacks are threatened.

But is all this defeatism? Both the incoming and the outgoing Moderators of the Kirk repeat what one hears from the leaders of so many denominations: that they are sure there is a vast army of the unchurched out there, believing in *something*, a bit vague about what, intensely interested in the person of Jesus but unenthusiastic about the organized Church. What's necessary, say the leaders, is evangelism – getting the good news of the Gospel to these people; and when they hear it, perhaps they will come to church – bringing, incidentally, their money with them.

Top church leaders, including the Archbishop of Canterbury, seem convinced that the makings of a national religious revival are there. I notice the American sociologist Daniel Bell saying much the same in his Hobhouse Memorial

Lecture at the London School of Economics, and as I said in an earlier note in this series, an astonishing number of ordinary people will admit to direct religious experience. But the problem remains of how to bring this spiritual life (if it really does exist) into the churches. What is keeping it out?

The outgoing Moderator of the Church of Scotland, the Very Reverend Professor Thomas Torrance, believes that the 3,000,000 Scots who are not on the rolls of any church have been 'pushed away from Christ' by the disunity within the churches. Myself, I wonder if this really counts for much. We all know people who say, 'I don't go to church because so-called Christians are no better than anyone else – they're hypocrites.' Boring services are another favourite scapegoat. And I have one friend who says what's put him off is being pestered for money all the time.

The Christian churches can hardly entertain the suggestion some humanists make, that the Christian faith itself is wanting, or at least needs some re-formulation. That being so there is, I think, one other factor that may count: the quality of the ministry itself. It is interesting that Dr Coggan, the Archbishop of Canterbury, should now challenge the fashion by saying that auxiliary, part-time ministers are *not* the panacea for the ills of the Church, and that there is no substitute for as large an army as possible of dedicated, full-time men and women workers. I am quite sure that the fathers and brethren in Edinburgh would growl 'Amen' to that. But if the ministry is the key, then both churches – of England and Scotland – must ask themselves, 'Are we attracting the best people to the ministry? Where is the talent going? If not to the churches, why not?'

Family Jubilee

4 June 1977

There is one aspect of all this year's jubilee jubilation that I hope we shall not overlook. We are celebrating not merely a reign but a family, a human continuity. This has started me thinking about the whole area of church and family – a relationship that ought, surely, to be an important aspect of our religious life, yet somehow gets neglected in a too-individualized approach to faith.

The Queen is probably untypical of today's mothers in having as many as four children. What sort of effect is our nationally declining birth rate going to have on the way we value our children, on how we educate and employ them? And, as the decline works its way up the ladder, upon the way we value and employ our old folk, too? In 1964 almost 1,000,000 babies were born in Britain. In 1975, fewer than 700,000. Should the churches stage a 'fertility drive', as it were? Or should they just try to adapt to circumstances? I can't help worrying, too, about the effect upon the human relations of society that a growing number of people brought up as only children may have. There's no doubt, in my experience, that people brought up in larger families are easier to live with.

The next thing that caught my eye is related: a vote by the postal workers' union to allow members to extend their working lives from sixty to sixty-five. Quite apart from reversing one of modern trade-unionism's most fashionable demands – a constantly falling retirement age in the interests of job-creation – this actually goes along with the insistence of bodies like Age Concern that the over-sixties do not necessarily want to be turned out to pasture earlier and earlier – they want to do something that the community values. And it seems to me there is a religious value here too, as there is with the children. For while there may be exceptions in certain cases – coal-mining underground, perhaps – it must be a kind of blasphemy to say that the faculties God gave us are of no further use after the age of sixty or fifty-five. Here, surely, is a case for treating people as individuals – a case against setting up hard and fast categories into which people have to be crammed whether they like it or not.

Battered wives, babies and even grannies have been in the news, too. Round it all up together and there's a great deal within the family to concern the churches – if, indeed, they *are* concerned with the family and not just with individual spirituality at one end of the scale and broad social values at the other. It is, after all, in this middle ground of family life that we meet those neighbours that we are supposed to be loving as we love ourselves.

I know that some faiths and churches do emphasize the family. Hinduism can be almost suffocatingly familial; the Mormon Church lays great emphasis on the weekly 'family home evening'. I know of one Roman Catholic archdiocese, in America, that specializes in week-end conferences at which married couples sort out their misunderstandings and renew their vows. And nobody can join a Jewish family for Sabbath without realizing that this is a family religion, and that the Eucharist is based upon a Jewish family meal, hymn-singing and all. One of the Jewish objections to taking Jesus as a model is, quite simply, that he was not a married man and, according to some readings, positively spurned his family. What kind of a son is that?

Personally, I think it is our restless Anglo-Saxon individualism, rather than our version of the Christian faith, that scatters our families and leaves them with weaker links together than most other societies. Many churches do indeed have some kind of council or guild focused upon the family, but I can't help noticing that they are often treated as rather fuddy-duddy women's work, while the men get on with the supposedly 'real' business of revising the liturgy or passing resolutions about politics. There are some fine exceptions, but in the long run, I don't see how church and family can be brought together effectively until the men – the fathers – take the subject seriously; until they go to church as conscientiously as their wives; until they throw their weight behind the traditionally women's issues and stop paying those terrible, arch compliments to the alleged youthfulness of the Women's League delegates.

So many problems of education, teenage unemployment, over-stressed young married people, wife-beating and retirement do lie within the family context. But it is a family which itself is often battered by the life it is obliged to lead. I am not entirely convinced by the Scots Moderator's argument that paying double time on Mondays instead of Sundays would help to restore family life by keeping the husbands at home – but I can see what he is getting at. The churches might do more to help and heal and lobby in this area, but they can only do so if they are equipped with adequate research and trained personnel. They have got to be sure of their facts and figures if they are going to take on the great bureaucracies.

Jesus in Kashmir

11 June 1977

I have just been reading a book by a young German philosopher – Andreas Faber-Kaiser – who considers it highly probable that Jesus did not die upon the cross – that he revived in the tomb, appeared naturally to his followers and then trekked eastwards through the Lost Tribes of Israel until he came to the Valley of Kashmir in northern India, where he settled down, got married, raised a family, died and was buried like anyone else. Herr Faber-Kaiser has visited the reputed tomb of Jesus, which he would like to have opened, and actually met one of our Lord's supposed descendants – a man of rare qualities, he thought.

Well, I have met Herr Faber-Kaiser, who is nice enough. But I must say, a bout with him is like arguing with someone who simply *knows* that Bacon wrote Shakespeare. There is no persuading them they may be mistaken, and yet, in the end, their thesis is strangely unimportant – a curious backwater that goes nowhere.

The book, *Jesus Died in Kashmir*, which Gordon and Cremonesi publish at £4.90, includes a massive bibliography and makes much reference to manuscripts in Persian and Sanskrit. I am afraid a good deal of this source material – like that dear old letter from Pontius Pilate to Tiberius Caesar, whose original, if you please, is always said to be lying, suppressed, in the Vatican Library – a good deal of it has long been assessed upon a scale ranging from dubious to spurious to pious fraud. To select one of the more remote titbits: there is said to be an account in Sanskrit of how, in the foothills of the Himalayas, a certain king encountered a fair-skinned Messiah who claimed to have been born of a virgin in a distant land. Faber-Kaiser thinks this was in A.D. 78 when Jesus would actually have been some eighty-five years of age. (Incidentally, the king is then supposed to have arranged the Messiah's marriage – but let that pass.) The difficulty is, as the author himself states, that 'the ancient history of India is mostly legendary and many mythical persons are treated as real'. Faber-Kaiser believes this particular chronicle to have been written in A.D. 115 – which is odd, seeing that the next chapter in it deals with a king who died about A.D. 1056, and one edition includes the Great Plague of 1899. It is, in short, a rather too flexible book to regard as a reliable record of history.

How do I know all this? Well, for one thing I have spent a number of weeks in Kashmir myself, and I have actually crawled about inside the supposed tomb. The custodian, naturally enough, was very ready to assure a visiting European of its authenticity. But the next thing is that I have read all this stuff before. For *I* have read, as Herr Faber-Kaiser assures me he has not – Robert Graves's and Joshua Podro's work, published twenty years ago, *Jesus in Rome*. Graves and Podro are selling a different theory – that Jesus died in Rome under the Emperor Claudius. But on their way to this conjecture they go through the Kashmir story almost exactly as Faber-Kaiser has it, and they point out the defects in the evidence.

It is clear – indeed it is admitted – that Faber-Kaiser has come to rely heavily upon the teachings of the Ahmadiya Muslims. These are a sect originating in Pakistan in the last century, but generally regarded as anathema and heretical to orthodox Islam. The Ahmadiya literature I have read refers respectfully to Jesus, but presents him as no more than a prophet, subsidiary even to the founder of the Ahmadiya movement, who is referred to as 'the promised Messiah'. A recent article in *The Times* went so far as to call the Ahmadiya 'essentially antichristian' and quite unscrupulous in their misinterpretation of Scripture. Certainly they have no interest in publishing anything that would verify the Christian Gospel.

Herr Faber-Kaiser himself tells me he is not a church member. He believes, he says, that God is too big for the mind to grasp, so you can't shake him by asking if he really believes the Holy Spirit would have allowed the churches to mislead the faithful all these years. And if you go on to ask, 'So Jesus deceived his disciples?' he answers 'yes'.

Some people will always go for the conspiracy theory. But the answer is, surely, that those hundreds of first Christians who were in a position to know the truth about Jesus did not act as if it were *that*. They behaved not as the disciples of one who had survived the cross and fled – but of one who died and rose again and is with us always.

The Saint of the Golden Breast

25 June 1977

This week's note is respectfully dedicated to the Diocese of Truro – whose centenary we are celebrating this year. I say 'we', because I dare to count myself as an honorary, if plastic, Cornishman, and because I reckon we don't hear enough about what Christianity in this country owes to the ancient Celtic Church and its noble army of neglected saints: St Ernie and St Issy and St Wenn, St Newan and St Nectan and St Teath, St Gluvias and St Veep, the disastrously named St Eval, the happy-sounding St Endellion and St Tewinoc, St Buryan and St Levan and, of course, St Senara.

I want to bring St Senara to the fore, not only because I am a part-time resident of her glorious parish of Zennor and therefore owe her some part-time devotion, but also because, by a fortunate coincidence, her recently-arrived vicar – the Reverend Canon Shane Cotter – has recently uncovered some old papers, compiled by the late Robert Morton Nance, which at last tell us something about our saint, of whom the guide-books used to boast 'nothing whatever is known'. (Mr Morton Nance, as Cornishmen will know, was a celebrated restorer and preserver of the old Cornish language during the years before the Second World War.)

As for Canon Cotter, he is rather appropriate too. In the days of the saints Cornwall's priests usually came to her from Brittany, Ireland or Wales. St Ia came to St Ives on a leaf; somebody else floating on a rock. Although Canon Cotter was translated, as it were, from a chaplaincy in Bahrain by the medium of British Airways, he is an undoubted Irishman. And this is the tale of St Senara, as revealed by his papers.

At the beginning of the sixth century A.D., the Count of León, in Brittany, had a beautiful daughter named Azenor. Note the resemblance to Senara and Zennor and do please accept it, because the entire value of this story turns on the assumption that they are one and the same. Well, one day the Count was out hunting with his daughter when a vicious serpent leapt upon him, fastened on the Count's arm and began to drain his life-blood away. Quick as a flash the brave Azenor bared her own fair bosom, whereupon the serpent (which knew a good thing when it saw one) let go of the Count and sank its fangs into the proffered decoy. And then, without hesitation, Azenor took her father's hunting knife, cut off her breast and flung it (with serpent attached) into the fire on which they had been cooking their lunch. As a reward for her piety (I suppose it counts as piety) heaven healed Azenor and rewarded her with a breast of gold.

But that is far from being the end. Our saint still has a long way to go, for in due course, Azenor was married to the King of Goello and the Count, her father, married a second time. The stepmother, jealous of Azenor's unique attractions, perhaps, accused the girl of infidelity. Azenor was thrown into a dungeon in the castle of Brest, under sentence to be burnt alive. There is, we are told, still a tower in the castle, though of a later date, known as 'the Tower of Azenor'. However, upon the discovery that the young Queen was to become a mother, she was not burnt but nailed up in a barrel and cast into the sea, so that her executioners might escape the charge of having murdered her unborn child.

Inside the barrel Azenor prayed to St Brigit, and there appeared to her an angel who ministered to her and fed her daily until, after five months, a son was born to her. Soon afterwards the barrel was driven ashore on the coast of Ireland. A thirsty kern was about to stave it with a rock, when the voice of a child, emerging through the bung, ordered him to have a care. He did. Mother and child stepped out, and the child grew up eventually to become the Abbot St Budoc, meaning 'the drowned one'. Apparently he despaired of the Irish, for, after some years, sought out by the penitent King of Goello, Budoc and his mother returned homewards. This time they used a stone coffin – nothing as humdrum as a boat for these saints – and are thought to have stopped on the way in Cornwall and to have founded mission cells there. Zennor would have been a very reasonable spot for one of them.

You may see St Budoc's arm in a silver reliquary somewhere in Brittany (why not his grandfather's, I wonder?). There are two or three dedications there to St Azenor, but *is* she the same as St Senara? At least there is no better candidate on record than the saint with the golden breast, who gave birth to another saint in a barrel.

And of what possible religious significance is all this

farrago? Well, I will say it again, that anything that reminds us of our first church – long before Augustine – deserves attention, for it was a jolly and holy church by all accounts. And should not every parish have some kind of myth to celebrate – its nod to our frankly pagan past?

Methodist Report

25 June 1977

We are now at the height of the annual church conference season. One after another the churches of the British Isles have been depositing fat volumes of reports – usually upwards of 400 pages long – upon my desk, where they land not always with a *dull* thud, because they are often full of interest if you know what not to read. The latest to land is the agenda for this year's Methodist Conference, which has just opened in Hull. I find it one of the best of them; though it might help delegates and reporters if Central Hall (the Methodist headquarters) would follow the Church of Scotland and issue the documents chapter by chapter over a period of weeks and not all in one lump, whence it is impossible to pick out more than a few plums – which I shall now try to do.

Over the past year Methodist districts and circuits have been pondering the Ten Propositions of the Churches' Unity Commission. Last year's conference advised a 'positive response'. But I guess it is a sign of the times that this year's report sums up the reactions as 'unenthusiastic acquiescence – a certain weariness', which it traces back to the disillusioning failure of the Anglican-Methodist unity scheme five years ago.

There is an interesting passage on broadcasting. The report says that four times as many people seem to be getting their religion from radio and television as get it from going to church. Does the future of the church lie with broadcasting? Is the church of the future going to be the church of the air? If so, the Methodist Division of Social Responsibility goes on to wonder what kind of Christianity the broadcasters are putting out. For 15,000,000 listeners (it says) they are the voice of Christianity, yet professional religious broadcasters are not appointed as representatives of the institutional Church, and (I quote this with a slight wince) 'they have little formal standing in church life'. *Touché!*

The Methodist Connexion has always been keen on homes for the aged, but now it notes a new trend in this direction. For the merely elderly, the emphasis is upon helping people to stay independent and in the community. But there are increasing numbers of very old and frail people, who need something much more than the kind of residential hotel that has been thought of as an old people's home up to now. Their numbers are far outstripping the resources of local authorities and the Health Service. Homes will have to adapt somehow to this need.

There has been a good deal of controversy over whether the Methodist Church (like the Society of Friends) should be running expensive fee-paying boarding schools – though they were not originally intended to be so exclusive. Perhaps the radical or so-called 'punk' Methodists will have something disturbing to say about that. Meanwhile, the Home Mission Division laments the changing pattern of life in the countryside. Once, agricultural workers were the backbone of the country chapel, while their masters, the farmers, attended the parish church. Today, Methodism is increasingly involved with the farmers, while the workers and their trade union keep away.

But I find that the most intriguing pages of the Blue Book report are those concerning the Methodist ministry itself. Like other churches, the Methodists are contemplating a part-time, unpaid auxiliary ministry. But, they wonder, will this downgrade the lay preacher and (at the same time) create a 'second-class ministry' of divided loyalty? Then there is a debate on the so-called 'sector ministry' – men and women who, instead of being marched up and down the country on church orders, are allowed to take up secular work in defined 'sectors' – as teachers, social workers, even broadcasters and parliamentary candidates. Is that true ministry, some wonder? Is it right, when the circuits are short of active ministers, that no fewer than 168 (6½ per cent of the total strength of the ministry) should be at desks and microphones instead of in the pulpit? One can't help wondering if there is not a little envy involved here, and how it can be reconciled with the demand for religious broadcasters to have standing in the Church.

Well, I have had my dig. But no one can fail to be moved by that part of the report which speaks of the psychological plight of all too many pastoral ministers – often under financial or family stress, uncertain of their usefulness or role, blaming themselves for the decline of their church. Who ministers to the minister? His own congregation, perhaps, who should not expect him to re-create some bygone golden age by the sheer power of his preaching.

Seven Against the Trinity

2 July 1977

Whenever one of these notes is devoted to views beyond the strictly orthodox, I get a fistful of letters telling me I have undermined the Christian faith and caused grief to thousands. That, I think, is to overrate my influence and to underrate the durability of the faith. Still, here we go again, I'm afraid.

Today's subject will scandalize the popular piety, not to mention that of many eminent divines as well. The Moderator of the Church of Scotland has already denounced the authors of this outrage as men who, 'if they were honourable would resign their professorships and divest themselves of their status as Christian ministers'. And spokesmen for the Archbishop of Canterbury have been diligently pointing out that two of those involved no longer hold the positions of influence within the Church of England attributed to them. Perhaps Lambeth is worried what the scandal will do to its standing with Rome and Istanbul.

I am talking, of course, about that controversial book *The Myth of God Incarnate*, published by the S.C.M. Press (the same stable as *Honest to God*) at £2.95. It is a collection of essays by seven mature and distinguished theologians including Don Cupitt (of Cambridge and some notoriety on television), Leslie Houlden (*former* Principal of Cuddesdon Theological College) and Maurice Wiles (*former* Chairman of the Church of England's Doctrine Commission). I dare say that, like the authors of the celebrated *Essays and Reviews* of 1860, they will be known as 'Seven Against The Trinity'.

In spite of the rather provocative use of the word 'myth' in the title, this is hardly a slick or sensational or even particularly original piece of work. The latter just goes to show the theological backwardness of the Church in this country – for which you may, if you will, say 'Thank goodness!' So in a way the book is more like a theologians' 'demo' – an attempt to put a message across to the public – than a great leap forward in Christian thinking. To put it in a dangerously neat nutshell, what they are saying is that Jesus did not claim to be the literal only son of God, and that the doctrine of Jesus as God in human flesh, the second person of the Trinity, is a myth in the sense of being a poetic or pictorial effort to express the meaning of Jesus, elaborated by those who had not actually known him personally. Don Cupitt says flatly that the doctrine of the incarnation distorts the message of Jesus, creating a cult of the divine Christ which has pushed the transcendent Father into the background, where Jesus never intended him to be.

But for many readers, I think the book's editor – Professor John Hick of Birmingham – will provide the most readily understood material. Many churchgoers will reject what he says with horror, but I think he is saying what many unchurched believers do in fact believe. And unless the churches can learn to speak their language, it will have to write them off at its peril. For I see the significance of this book as a bridge towards the unchurched believer.

Professor Hick is an expert in oriental religions, and this has convinced him that a God who loves all his creation cannot possibly have appointed Jesus as the one and only way to salvation. And he argues that New Testament scholarship today does not maintain that Jesus claimed he ever was such a way. John Hick says, 'Jesus was possibly the most wonderful human being that ever lived – one intensely open to God. He is not the property of the Christian Church.'

Simply 'the most wonderful human being'? Well, Jesus is not the property of John Hick either, of course. *The Myth of God Incarnate* is by no means immune to criticism, and a team of rival theologians, including a Roman Catholic bishop, is hard at work already on a refutation of what they call its 'damaging and misleading arguments'. They will, no doubt, demand how it is possible that for 1,900 years the Church could have been seeing things in the Bible that were not there. Then they will themselves have to answer this: is the doctrine of the Trinity to be found, explicitly and emphatically, in the New Testament? And where?

It seems to me, peering through the smoke of battle, that God may not change but that, as we move through time, men surely do. And as our position changes we must see different aspects of the unchanging. If there is a God, he must be infinite. No human language will ever define him. All talk about him must be in the nature of metaphor, poetry, myth. Is it really so surprising, so intolerable, that a new aspect of Jesus should now come into view?

But first Hans Küng – now this! Some will say such Christians are no Christians. Stand by for the counter-attack!

The Black Presence in Synod

9 July 1977

The General Synod of the Church of England has just committed itself to a very solemn statement of belief which, having been considerably amended in debate, it may be as well to assemble here in one piece. It reads as follows: 'This Synod recognizes that the emergence of a society which comprises different racial, cultural and religious groups lays upon the Church the duty to use the opportunity for the enrichment of our national and personal life.'

The parliamentary process has not made the meaning exactly crystal clear, so let me pick out two or three important implications. First, that the Church of England is positively accepting and even welcoming the fact that Britain is now an irreversibly multiracial society. And it welcomes that, both because it sees here opportunities for the Church, and because it believes the newcomers can enrich and refresh our old way of life. And the Church is welcoming not just the cultural and racial gifts (perhaps it is too soon yet to hear about the positive benefits of interracial marriage) but also the gifts of religious refreshment. It was, I think, the Bishop of Winchester who insisted that our minorities had their religious rights as well as social and economic ones that must be recognized.

The Synod's debate was rooted in some thorough documentation, not all of which, I suspect, got read by members. In particular, there was a report from the British Council of Churches, *The New Black Presence in Britain*. This is a severe and uncompromising piece of work which leaves little room for escape from some radical and political conclusions. It makes the positive case for multiracialism by pointing out that the new black communities have a vigorous, fertile and irrepressible imagination which a stagnant and cynical Britain badly needs.

The report says that the main cause of racial friction is

not the arrival of black people, but something more deeply rooted in the nature of our society. The blacks are holding up to us a mirror in which we can see features that were here long before they arrived. Is it possible for British society to operate except as a heap of people struggling for success, in which somebody has to be at the bottom of the pile to make success credible? In effect, the report blames British isolationism. Because we are trapped by our past into defending a doubtful inheritance of supposed cultural and economic superiority, we can no longer see the truth about ourselves in comparison with other peoples.

And that, I take it, is what the Bishop of Truro, Dr Leonard, had in mind when he said that Christians should not neglect the prophetic for the expedient – must not blur the Gospel that human ills can only be solved by redemption in Christ and the re-creation of man. It was a defiantly theological speech that refused to justify the Church's stand on political, economic or sociological grounds, but insisted upon Christian truths first and foremost. That God has created all men in his own image, and that we must love our neighbour – black or white – without exception. That God has created a world of rich diversity, and that it is a heresy to think that equality must mean identity – which is why a policy of trying to assimilate Asians and Africans and remould them 'just like us' must be rejected. And that God is always trying to draw the best from people, and that their full potential will only be realized if they are willing to listen to each other and learn.

Well, you may say, that's a nice theory for a bishop, especially one whose throne is in as pleasant a place as Truro. It is different in Bradford and Barnet, and the Bishop of Edmonton, Bill Westwood, has an uncomfortable way of pointing out facts that don't fit in with the theories: like schools where the English kids share the bottom of the heap with the West Indians while the Hindus and Cypriots go to the top. (Parental influence to thank is my guess – the English have a low opinion of education.)

But it is different, too, in Washington D.C., where David Sheppard, Bishop of Liverpool, was astonished recently to find blacks at the top of the tree in their professions, including the episcopal church. 'In Liverpool,' he says, 'we've had a black community since the 1890s. But eighty years later, black managers, teachers, clergy are scarcely to be seen. People say, "If only you wouldn't make so much noise about race relations this progress you want would happen easily". Well,' says Bishop Sheppard, 'Liverpool gives the lie to such bland optimism. We haven't – and it hasn't.'

Blasphemy

16 July 1977

So blasphemy is back in fashion, if indeed it ever went out. What I mean is, first the Church of England General Synod carries a resolution deploring blasphemy on the air; next *Gay News* is found guilty in the first case of its kind for more than half a century. The last time a case like it was heard was 1921, and the accused got nine months' hard labour for comparing Christ to a circus clown. Under Old Testament law, Byzantine law and Scots law (until the eighteenth century) blasphemy was a crime punishable by death.

I imagine the severity of the sentence was dictated by the belief that the entire community was liable to be punished by heaven for the sins of the blasphemer – 'Shut him up before we all suffer for it'. And the prosecution case against *Gay News* made it perfectly clear that there is still a strong element of preserving the security of the State, rather than the good name of the Deity. The judge confirmed that all that was necessary was to show that the blasphemy might cause a breach of the peace by arousing angry feelings among the faithful. So it was all much less a matter of theology than of hypothetical law and order, about which English law is always very sensitive. You might think we were one of the world's most volatile and unruly peoples.

But several other elements were involved too – whether or

not they were meant to be. Good taste was involved. I personally feel it showed a lack of sensitivity to circulate the poem in public. As *The Times* remarked, 'Few followers of the Christian religion, even those lukewarm in their devotion, could have been anything but utterly revolted by it.'

The case also involved attitudes towards homosexuality as such. Here I find myself caught between a compassion which I know I ought to feel, and a certain negative feeling of which I honestly am not ashamed. The thing is, I am not terribly interested in homosexuality, any more than I am in, say, cricket or horses, and I don't feel inclined to join in any great campaign for or against it. Certainly I number homosexuals among my friends and whatever their private joys and problems may be, I greatly respect the way they keep them to themselves and don't bother or offend me with them. I am glad to thank heaven for sparing *me* such problems, but I simply don't feel qualified or provoked into joining that particular battle myself. Freudians may make what they will of that.

Prosecution has given the offending poem a circulation it would not otherwise have had, I am sure. All the same, there are a number of implications that Christians ought to consider. Is it right, in an increasingly multicultural society, that only Christians should be so protected? Muslims and Sikhs might be far more easily aroused to break the peace in protest at blasphemy against their prophets. And if private persons have the right to bring prosecutions of this kind, where should it end? Is it possible, is it desirable, that ways should be sought of enforcing all of the Ten Commandments through the courts? Should the churches sponsor such prosecutions?

The other day, I had a sad little postcard from an old age pensioner who had taken his wife to see a film called *Emanuelle*, on the assumption it would be about Jesus, only to find it was, as he put it, 'Naked women making love to women'. Almost every society (and particularly Communist ones, as it happens) requires *some* inhibitions to be exercised in public, and I don't think it can reasonably be denounced as illiberal, oppressive or unchristian for doing so. Personally, I have doubts about whether punishment works, but I do think a society is entitled to make certain gestures to show it does not approve of certain behaviour – wants to dissociate itself from it. Those gestures ought not to be cruel and unusual, and the term 'society' ought to imply a pretty wide consensus. But a nation has the need to express itself.

On top of the censorship issue, *is* blasphemy a proper subject for such expressions? It seems that only 29 per cent of the population believe in a personal God, and yesterday's blasphemy is tomorrow's hit musical. One can only conclude that it is up to the people and the juries on which they serve. (Ah, but how are juries selected?) It may also be up to the churches which ought to be teaching and nurturing the people. For it seems to me that if obscene and blasphemous libels *are* publicly printed, and not inhibited by the manners, morals and taste of the day, it is because there is no longer a public consensus on what those manners, morals and taste should be. The Church used to be the strongest single influence in building them. Why is it so no longer? Should something else take its place?

Never on Sabbath

23 July 1977

I know a man who really tries to live by the Ten Commandments. The hardest, he finds, is the one against bearing false witness. To him that means no office gossip. The one he is most thankful for is the fourth – no working on Sundays, whatever the excuse. Did I say 'Sunday'? But of course the Bible says 'Sabbath' or 'seventh day', which is Saturday. But to distinguish themselves from the Jews, early Christians kept Sunday, the day he rose again from the dead, as the Lord's Day. It was certainly a very different affair from the orthodox Jewish Sabbath, with a strong emphasis on community and doing good works.

In A.D. 321 the Christian Emperor Constantine decreed a weekly holiday 'upon the venerable day of the Sun' – though it was compulsory only for city-dwellers. Down through the ages there have been exemptions for country folk, partly because of their incorrigible paganism, partly because of the demands of the beasts and crops.

Increasingly the Church began to justify the restrictions of Sunday by reference to the Old Testament. The book of Numbers cites an example of the death penalty for Sabbath-breaking. Instead of a positive Lord's Day, we acquired a rather negative Christian Sabbath, which had not been the original idea at all. In late Saxon England it was observed from 3 p.m. on Saturday until dawn on Monday. But there seems to have been a steady undercurrent of popular resistance. Cornwall is full of circles of granite 'maidens', turned to stone for dancing on Sunday.

Along comes the Reformation. Luther maintained that the fourth commandment was essentially a Jewish ritual law which had been abrogated by the new covenant of Christ. Christians, he declared, must be lords of the Sabbath. Even Calvin was more flexible in the matter than you might imagine – he went bowling on Sunday afternoons. John Knox was not at all averse to party-going on Sundays. It seems to have been Puritan ideas imported from England that really robbed the Scots Sabbath of its fun.

One effect of the Reformation in England was to abolish vast numbers of saints' days. The English now found themselves working harder than they had ever done, so they tended to let rip on the remaining Sundays, with all kinds of gluttony, drunkenness, cricket-playing and worse. One seventeenth-century divine complains of 'smooching and groping'.

Now there is nothing our ruling classes have always feared more than workers with time on their hands. The moment work stops, disorder is liable to break out. Poring over their newly-acquired English Bibles, the bourgeoisie concluded that six days' labour was compulsory, to be followed by a seventh of full-time holiness. This was the covenant that the Lord's people must keep, and it served very well, too, as the framework for a disciplined industrial society. Even games after church were discouraged. The Puritans feared they were irrational and appealed to man's appalling lower nature.

Failing to build the Kingdom of God in England, the Puritans moved on to the uncorrupted shores of North America – the chosen people in covenant for the promised land. And it is here that I must reveal my debt to a splendid book, *Redeem the Times* by Winton Solberg, which Harvard University Press has published at the shuddering price of £12.95. It deals with the Puritan Sabbath in early America, and it is crammed with scholarly chapter and verse.

Since everyone was expected to attend worship, absentees had the opportunity for all kinds of unbroadcastable naughtiness, and the penalties for Sabbath sinning were enhanced. Adultery on the Sabbath was severely punished, more so than on other days of the week. Even holding hands under apple-trees was an offence. And the penalty for burglary during divine worship was to be branded with the letter B on the forehead and to have one ear cut off.

We meet, too, in this volume such admirable characters as the Rogerenes and the Ephrata Dunkers – a community of Baptist monks and nuns who reverted to the Jewish Sabbath, vowed chastity and engaged in love-feasts and foot-washing. And the Red Indians who, when exhorted to rest on the Sabbath replied, 'It is a small thing, for we have not much to do on *any* day.'

It is easy enough to laugh at Sabbatarianism. Perhaps it did tend to suppress the healthily playful side of man and to wall off religion from the rest of life. But it did serve a genuine social purpose and it encouraged people to devote just a little time to higher things. One is reminded of Voltaire: 'If you wish to destroy the Christian religion you must first destroy Sunday.' And we very nearly have.

The Irish Problem

30 July 1977

The Church of England's Board for Social Responsibility is sticking its neck further and further out these days. Under its chairman, Dr Graham Leonard (Bishop of Truro), and its go-ahead young secretary, Giles Ecclestone (who used to be one of the clerks in the House of Commons), the Board has presented two challenging documents for discussion in just over a month.

The first was *Britain as a Multi-racial and Multi-cultural Society* which managed to offend some listeners to this programme by its tolerant attitude to other faiths. Now comes *The Irish Problem and Ourselves*, a compact discussion paper by Mr Ecclestone and Canon Eric Elliott of Belfast, which, it is hoped, will be thoroughly talked about at the diocesan level before the big debate at Church House in November.

The main news point has been broadcast elsewhere already: the recommendation that British Christians should lobby their M.P.s and Government to resume political negotiations on the future of Northern Ireland. The discussion paper thinks it intolerable that Westminster should go on treating the Northern Irish like colonials, imposing a moratorium on ordinary politics and denying them any representative institutions except on Westminster's 'stand-pat' view of power-sharing. Well, you might say, any political party could have come up with that. What business is it of the Church of England?

Here Dr Leonard (a High-Churchman, incidentally) justifies the paper emphatically. People are too ready to say, 'Well, I could try this or that – but frankly all I can do is pray for you.' What they *should* say is, 'First and foremost I'll pray – then I will try this and that.' So the object of this paper (says the bishop) is informed prayer: we want to rid people of the temptation either to wash their hands of the problem, or to react angrily against it. And Giles Ecclestone rejects the fashionable contention that to talk in terms of Catholic and Protestant is simply to use religious titles for what is really secular, political conflict. Of course there are important historic, economic and social dimensions to it all, but there is also a religious aspect. The Church in Ireland plays a rather different role from that in England. It has subtly fed the situation in the past, and it still has the power to change it in the future.

The Elliott-Ecclestone paper underlines several reasons why British Christians should now grasp the nettle of Ireland – not least that the Irish churches themselves have asked us to. Further, it says, the Ulster problem is 'a legacy of England's tragic and bloody involvement', and in view of the long history of injustice visited by Britain upon Ireland, it may be that reconciliation can only be brought about by an explicit and symbolic expression of repentance on Britain's part – something that perhaps only the churches are capable of expressing. The implications of this – a solemn, national confession of guilt, even a penitential pilgrimage – these deserve to be turned into action and not just played with as good ideas in principle. The Peace People have blazed the trail.

But you can't accuse the paper of being soft on Catholics. It points out the damaging effects upon any chance of Irish unity that have been inflicted by Church dictation to the State in matters like contraception, education, censorship, mixed marriage and divorce. By breaking the link with the Commonwealth and then developing Ireland as a Catholic, Gaelic-speaking republic, Dublin has offered no reassurance whatever to the fears of northern Protestants.

The study paper also takes a line which is not going to please those who denounce so-called institutional violence. The authors recognize that it is fashionable in some circles to justify violent action in pursuit of justice and liberation. But, they say, Ireland has shown that an emotional investment in violence may only perpetuate that violence. Responsible citizens must support the civil power against all paramilitary forces, as an essential prerequisite of progress to a political settlement. There should be no 'Let's cut our losses and bring the Army home'.

So what now? What after the General Synod has debated this? The paper calls for informed prayer and for contributions to the various funds for reconciliation in Ireland, funds which (in my view) have been wretchedly neglected by British church people. And maybe the bishops will indeed lobby their friends at Westminster for a new political initiative. But it will be interesting to see if the churches in Britain really can bring themselves to make that explicit and symbolic expression of repentance for our sins against Ireland.

The World Council

6 August 1977

I am recording this in what would appear to be a large comprehensive school in the north-west suburbs of Geneva, with a view of oak-trees, a field of maize and three small brown and white cows upon which it has been raining heavily. In fact I am at the Ecumenical Centre, headquarters of the World Council of Churches, whose Central Committee has been meeting here this week past.

There are those who say that if the World Council of Churches did not exist, it would be quite unnecessary to invent it. I must say I take the opposite view. I am not sure I would invent this particular World Council, but I think Christendom does need some sort of international forum for two important reasons: first as a place in which to hammer away at the question of its own disunity. You may wonder whether unity in the strict sense of the word is quite as important as some ecumenists make out. To quote Lukas Vischer, the World Council's leading ecumenical technician: 'It is often said today that the goal of full communion is unrealistic; that it is enough for the churches to understand each other and to be prepared to co-operate with each other. Diversity is praised in a way that amounts in fact to the justification of division. Unity is dismissed as uniformity.'

But, Dr Vischer insists, 'The churches must be able to recognize one another wholly and unreservedly as churches of Christ. On the basis of the one common faith and baptism, they must be able to celebrate the Eucharist together.' This raises quite enough in the way of agenda, not least for those like the Quakers and Salvationists who have no sacraments, yet insist they are truly Christian.

But it seems to me the other big reason for having a World Council is to provide somewhere where the old white churches – the dying churches, you might be tempted to call them – are exposed to the impact of the young brown, black and yellow churches, many of which are vital with the life that comes only from suffering and persecution. To Christians like these, our obsessions with *Gay News* or *The Myth of God Incarnate* are utterly meaningless. They want to know what we are going to do about Rhodesia, torture in Latin America, the cynical materialism of the arms trade and the multinational corporations which they suspect are pillaging and cheating their homelands. And you don't impress these people by telling them to stop playing the Communist game and become more spiritual. Their parishioners are very simple working folk, and if 'Thy Kingdom come, on Earth' doesn't mean 'Let there be peace and justice for the poor', then our sort of religion really is nothing more to them than the opiate of the masses.

When you think how long churches have supported unjust and cruel authority, it is remarkable that some parts of the world have any Christians left at all, and far from surprising that a Cuban Christian should declare, 'We are confessing Christ when we work together with the Marxists to build a new society.' It was a Czech who said that Christians in his country were obliged to confess Christ by the style of life they were seen by all around them to be leading. How about your style of life? And mine?

Of course some of this talk is politically dutiful. One would hardly expect the official Russian Baptist to do other than denounce the neutron bomb. The World Council may also be too much identified with its Secretary, Dr Philip Potter. Some of its reports may be shallow and its staff are often obliged to bite off more than they are qualified or equipped to chew. But I don't think a World Council of Churches would be worth much if it were *not* anti-capitalist and anti-imperialist in the best sense of those terms – unless you think churches are just stone buildings for use on Sundays.

I think the Council suffers from the academic and extremely expensive setting of Geneva, which is not to say it would be better off in London as an alternative. The typical British manner is not popular at the Council. As I have said before, we are regarded as patronizing, penny-pinching, only interested in human rights as a tit for tat against charges of racism. Our calls for economy, our plea of national poverty, our less than generous subscriptions to World Council appeals are not well-regarded. Dr Coggan's visit here last May opened no new era – which is a pity.

The Truth of the Myth

10 September 1977

Just over two months ago, I reviewed a work by Professor John Hick and others, *The Myth of God Incarnate*. Its general thesis was that Jesus did not really claim to be the literal only son of God, and that the doctrine of him as God in human flesh, the second person of the Trinity, was at best a myth – in the sense of being a poetic effort to express his meaning – at worst, a distortion which has pushed into the background the transcendent Father whom Jesus himself worshipped.

I said at the time that Professor Hick and his colleagues were saying what many unchurched believers do in fact believe. But, I added, it was going to shock a great many sincere, traditional church members – which indeed it did. The initial response from people like Professor James Atkinson was to denounce the authors as 'theological cripples', but to refrain from taking them on at their own level of seriousness.

I am still not sure they have been accorded that courtesy. Hodder Christian Paperbacks have now issued, at 80p, the promised rebuttal. It is entitled *The TRUTH of God Incarnate* and is based, somewhat ignobly, upon a set of proofs of *The Myth* retrieved, we are told, from an Oxford dustbin.

The result is not exactly rubbish – how could it be with such distinguished contributors as Canon Michael Green (the editor), Bishop Stephen Neill, Professor John McQuarrie, the Reverend Brian Hebblethwaite and Roman Catholic Bishop Christopher Butler? – but it still has a certain crumpled quality about it.

Bishop Butler and Dean Hebblethwaite have both contributed succinct and sober essays, entirely free of undignified personal polemics. But I am afraid the same is not true of the two major contributors, Bishop Neill and Canon Green. This is a special pity in the bishop's case because he has a number of good points to make. But they are accompanied by some rather patronizing personal references to the 'mythologists' and a good deal of academic name-dropping. What the bishop is trying to do, as I understand him, is to dismiss the Hickites as too immature to realize that their warmed-up unitarianism has all been considered and dismissed before. What we are being offered in *The Myth*, it appears, is little better than the Arian heresy which was sorted out at the Council of Chalcedon in A.D. 451.

Canon Michael Green, of course, is a leading conservative Evangelical. His contributions, rather more than half the book, have a strongly propagandistic tone. Fair enough, if you can take it in that spirit (so often deplored by churchmen when journalists display it) – hard-hitting, sensational, even a trifle slanted at times. For example: 'I asked a friend who he thought would have written a book with such a title as *The Myth of God Incarnate*. He replied "the Communists!"' A foul blow, perhaps? Communists, having read their Sorel, would at least be prepared to grant Professor Hick's legitimate definition of 'myth' – and not that of 'fairy-tale' which Canon Green and company are so determined to foist upon him. But once again, some strong points are made here and there.

Canon Green takes up squarely the challenge to identify those places in the New Testament where the doctrines of the Trinity and the divinity of Christ are to be found, though he passes over many others which leave Jesus firmly subordinate to the Father. It is true, I think, that *The Myth* fails to deal convincingly with the resurrection, or with the objection that the sternly monotheistic Jews were the last people on earth one might have expected to produce an incarnation of their God. But I am not sure it is wise to lean too heavily on the centurion's 'Truly this man was the Son of God', when all the modern translations prefer '*a* son of God'.

Personally, I should have thought the biggest objection to *The Myth* argument lies in experience. It seems completely meaningless to those churches which are most alive and vigorous today, the churches of Africa, Latin America and Eastern Europe.

I don't fancy Canon Green's curious comparison with dismantling a motor car, but I can see that the stripped-down Christianity of *The Myth* school does lack the richness, the mystery, the magic that many worshippers long for. Nevertheless, it seems to me that you cannot just cry 'Reductionism! Arianism! Unitarianism!' as if that alone could win the argument. Why do these 'heresies' keep coming back after all these years? Surely it is because they do speak to the condition of many people who have a direct apprehension of God, quite free of Nicene or Chalcedonian complications. Must such people embrace confusion?

It is good that Bishop Stephén Neill should end his contribution, 'We are scattered vessels of his fleet. Yet we can salute one another in passing . . . And we can hope that, in the infinite mercy and goodness of God, we may all in the end safe within the harbour meet.'

Shrouded in Mystery

17 September 1977

For journalists, there has not been a religious story to match it since the supposed tomb of St Peter was found in Rome. Here in London, a gathering of distinguished clergy and scientists, ranging from *Honest to God* John Robinson to a pair of space doctors from the United States Air Force, all finding it well nigh impossible to resist the conclusion that the Holy Shroud of Turin is indeed the linen cloth in which the body of Christ was entombed.

If true, the shroud ought to be about the holiest object in Christendom. Yet it is many centuries since it was authorized by the Church for popular veneration, and the Vatican has only recently begun to tone down its view of it as a pious fraud. Relics have long had a shady reputation, and the Thirty-nine Articles still refer scathingly to 'The Romish doctrine concerning relics . . . grounded upon no warranty of Scripture'. Still, it is part of the shroud case that this relic is fully and uniquely grounded in Scripture – science is said to bear that out. The weakest links are the historical ones.

The first thing we know for sure about this fourteen-foot-long strip of linen is that it was placed in a church in French Savoy by one Geoffrey de Charny – a man with close Crusader connections – in 1353. Now, the Crusaders had looted Constantinople in 1204, and there were subsequent tales of the Knights Templar venerating a bearded male head. We do know that, prior to the sacking of Constantinople, one of the city's chief treasures was just such an image known as the *Mandylion*. This had been acquired at great cost (and some threatening) from the Syrian city of Edessa, in the year 942. Again, there are tales further back still of a portrait of Jesus 'not made with hands' being in Edessa as early as the first century. With the persecution of the Christians it disappeared, to be rediscovered sealed in the city wall some time in the sixth century. That is supposed to be what the Byzantines bought. But was it the same as the shroud we have now – let alone the same as the original shroud?

The present relic was moved to the Royal Chapel of Savoy in Turin in 1478, charred by narrowly escaping destruction in a fire. The last time it was publicly exhibited was 1933, and with some reluctance the church authorities agreed to show it again in 1978, the fifth centenary of its arrival in Turin. This was fervently welcomed by the growing world-wide fraternity of shroud enthusiasts, who determined to hold an international conference there in the hopes of being allowed to examine the very fabric itself. For the conclusions they have reached so far are based largely upon photographs.

It was the very first picture, taken in 1898, that revealed that the image upon the cloth was far more compelling than had been realized before. For it turns out to be, in negative, the representation of a naked, crucified body – the face of an archetypal Christlikeness – showing many details of torment and execution which do not accord with Renaissance and medieval stereotypes, but are confirmed by modern research. For example, the nails on the shroud go through the wrists, not through the palms of the hands where they could not, in fact, have supported the body's weight.

The more the images are exposed to computer enhancement, image analysis and projection into three dimensions, the harder it is to see how they could have been faked. There appear to have been coins placed over the eyelids. If only their impressions could be deciphered, the dating might prove sensational. As it is, examination of pollen particles and linen weave confirm that it just could be first-century Palestinian. As for exact identity, who else was flogged, crucified in a cap of thorns and dispatched with a spear-thrust close to the heart?

But there is still room for doubters. Is it not a shade too good to be true? Just how was the image produced – by some nuclear flash? And if it is, in some sense, a print from being folded over a solid form, why is the image not distorted when flattened out?

Some sceptics connect the current rush of shroud publicity with the making of a film about it by a young Englishman, David Rolfe. Rolfe himself says that everyone who has worked on the film has become increasingly excited and convinced. Well, maybe it is time to refresh our belief in the real, historical Christ. And maybe it is appropriate, a kind of divine irony, that science, having destroyed so much faith, should be enlisted to restore it.

But for myself, I cannot help feeling that, however genuine, the shroud can tell us nothing we do not already know – that it may even prove an idolatrous red herring across the painful path of living the Christian life.

To Russia With Love

24 September 1977

The Archbishop of Canterbury is off on his visit to Moscow, the Ukraine and Armenia. Following his trips earlier this year to India and the Pacific, to Rome, Geneva and Istanbul, there are some in the Church who wish he would stay at home and pay more attention to his domestic flock. Yet Dr Coggan is the leader, so to speak, of the world-wide Anglican Communion, which will be conferring next summer at Canterbury, so there is a good case for his gathering his own ecumenical experience.

I think it is important to rid the Russian visit of any patronizing implications. Dr Coggan is not going prison visiting, or bearing theological enlightenment to the backward. On the contrary, it is most likely he will draw from Russia considerable spiritual enrichment. At least two of his accompanying counsellors speak Russian and know the Orthodox Church, and as one of them told me, 'The nearest I have ever been to heaven is hearing the liturgy at the great monastery of Zagorsk.' Well, Dr Coggan will be visiting Zagorsk – and Etchima Dzin, the holy city of the Armenians, whose survival and vigour should on no account be overlooked.

It is not just the magic of the Russian liturgy, though this has an importance which it is almost impossible for Westerners to grasp, and for which the Orthodox will make almost any sacrifice to keep it going. It is also the sheer miracle of the Church's survival at all in the face of so much brainwashing and anti-religious propaganda. It is a fact almost to be envied, that the Church grows stronger when it is up against downright atheism than when it is surrounded by indifference, as it is in Britain. Here it costs nothing to be a Christian. You are not ridiculed for going to church, not excluded from college, thrown off the housing lists or dismissed from your job. But a believer in the Soviet Union must really stand up and be counted. Everyone Dr Coggan meets, Orthodox, Baptist, Armenian and Jew, will have made that defiant gesture.

The Soviet Government always claims that nobody is persecuted for religious belief, only for breaking the law. The law happens to require State approval of all congregations and appointments within them, and to forbid any activities outside the holding of services within the church building: no youth clubs, no Bible classes, no racks of pamphlets for people to take home. For while atheist propaganda is organized by the State as part of the educational system, the churches are forbidden to answer back or evangelize.

I am sure Dr Coggan is well aware of all this, and of the 2,000 or so Christians who are said to be in labour camps or psychiatric hospitals. The Archbishop is certainly not afraid of speaking his mind, but he is also aware that if the doors are to be kept open between the Russian churches and the outside world (as the Russian churches desperately want them to be), then the Soviet Government must not be given any excuse for slamming them shut. Experience indicates that continual private expressions of concern – showing you know what is really going on in the Soviet Union – are more helpful, if less headline-hitting, than making a public outcry. The Russian churches are growing fast, often full to overflowing. But in spite of Helsinki the hierarchy is fearful that, if provoked, the State could launch yet another wave of persecution that would stamp out the liturgy altogether.

In any case, Dr Coggan has plenty of ecclesiastical business on his hands. The Orthodox Church regards itself, not Rome, as the one true church whose doctrines and rituals require no reform or updating. Ecumenical conversations with the Anglicans are less a matter of both converging upon some distant truth than of the Orthodox enquiring to determine how near to their own eternal standards the Anglicans come. On the matter of women priests, they fear we are falling too far short to justify any further discussion. Some warning shots will probably be fired across the bows of the Lambeth Conference. The Orthodox have great difficulty in understanding the devolution and synodical form of government of the Anglican churches.

There will not, however, be any dramatic breaking off of inter-church relations. As with the Baptists and the Armenians, this is essentially an exercise in brotherhood and in the joyful affirmation of resurrection – that Christ is risen indeed!

Epoch-Making at Mohonk

1 October 1977

The word went out into first-century Judaea: 'Repent, repent, for the Kingdom of Heaven is at hand – indeed, is already upon you!' And parables were told to illustrate what the Kingdom was like.

This past week I have been here in the United States listening to a strangely similar message. Though perhaps, in the end, the message was less strange than the place and the people involved.

The people were some forty journalists and international development experts drawn from North America, Britain, Africa, India and Australia, for the most part. The place deserves a more thorough description. It is a rambling resort hotel in the Catskills, known as Mohonk Mountain House. Founded in 1869 by a Quaker family called Smiley (who still run the place) it has had a long tradition as a base for conferences on questions like international peace and arbitration, Indian affairs and respect for nature.

The setting almost suggests the subjects, for it is one of the most calm and beautiful I have ever been in. The house itself is a bit grotesque by English standards, like a cross between a Victorian hospital and the Viceregal Lodge in Simla. It is better to be inside it looking out than the other way round. For outside are two equally sublime but quite different views: to one side, a lake with limestone cliffs and pinewoods, that might almost have been designed for some production of Wagner's *Ring*; to the other, a wide valley with mountains rising and falling along the distant skyline.

But what has this to do with our Religious Affairs Correspondent and his work? It does not make much better sense when I add that we were all conferring on the subject of 'Media Values and the Third World' – which might be translated, 'Do Western newspapers and broadcasting give a square deal to Asia, Africa and Latin America?'

This happens to be something that I see as a religious and moral issue, since if you believe in the universal fatherhood of God it must be a kind of blasphemy to abuse and misrepresent your fellow men. But what gave the conference another level of religious significance was the presence – the presidency – of a secular prophet crying once more, 'Repent, repent, the Kingdom is already upon us and this is what it is like!'

The name of this prophet should not be unfamiliar to you – Dr Jonas Salk, discoverer of the first (and he believes still the best) polio vaccine. He is a warm, bright, elf-like man who has devoted much of his time and money since to the financing of humane studies and 'think-tanks' like the one in California that was graced by the late Dr Jacob Bronowski.

Dr Salk has recently created something that he calls the 'Epoch B Foundation', deriving its title from his own book *The Survival of the Wisest*, in which he argues that human beings have reached 'Epoch B', a stage in evolution in which (if they are to survive) co-operative and non-violent attitudes must replace competitive and aggressive ones such as have characterized the struggle to survive in the previous epoch, 'Epoch A'.

The concept of 'A' and 'B' is less arbitrary than it sounds when one sees Dr Salk explaining it with the charts and graphs that his scientific background brings naturally to his fingers. In particular, there is the so-called 'sigmoid curve', a long, shallow S-shape, which helps him to explain that things like population do not go on increasing faster and faster for ever, but, even as they climb, reach a 'point of inflection' at which they start to tilt the other way, slow down and flatten out.

Jonas Salk thinks we are genetically programmed to do this – that in the case of population, it is inevitable, but that we can influence the inevitable by adopting attitudes that are in harmony with it, instead of discordant to it. What might have been a positive value in 'Epoch A' may turn out to be of negative value in 'Epoch B'. So it is not a case of the 'survival of the fittest' in the old sense, since the fittest for 'A' will resist the change to 'B'. It is probably the weakest who want the change. It is the minority, the mutant, who must be given their chance, and in fact are going to survive anyway. Blessed are the meek, the humble, the poor – they will inherit the Earth.

It is hard to go much further without Dr Salk's graphs to point to. I can imagine a Marxist tearing the theory apart as élitist, bourgeois, sentimental, and an Evangelical condemning it for leaving out Christ. But I can also imagine Teilhard de Chardin and probably Richard Acland nodding their agreement with the 'Epoch B' theory.

What I found especially intriguing was to watch Jonas Salk constructing what is virtually a theology – a view of the present and coming kingdom – without the use of the word God. In conversation with him, I find this does not bother either of us. Jonas Salk certainly *thinks* God and apprehends God. 'What a pity,' he says, 'that man has gone and made God supernatural.'

Expository Times

8 October 1977

In my youth, there was a magazine called *Fur & Feather – Incorporating the Amateur Aquarist and Reptilian Gazette.* It was a splendid title, and in the same spirit I cherish that of my latest reading matter, *The Expository Times.* This, I know, sounds as if it ought to be monumentally dull. But it is not, and this year it has been publishing a rewarding series of articles under the heading 'Living in a Multicultural Society'. Fur and feather, indeed, for among the articles are those by a Jew, a Hindu, a Muslim and a Sikh, all looking critically at Christianity in a way that Christians seldom dare.

It should not be too strange to hear what the Jewish writer, Rabbi Dov Marmur, of a London Reform Synagogue says. And yet I have my doubts whether many Christians will really want to bear in mind what he has to say – that the churches still have not really washed their hands of anti-Semitism, that they still have not given up hope of converting Israel to the one true (Christian) faith.

Rabbi Marmur tells the dreadful story of being approached by a lady who demanded of him, 'We Christians have the Ten Commandments. Do you Jews have something comparable?' And he goes on to complain that in spite of the obvious positive influence of Pharisaic Judaism on early Christianity, the churches still appear to stand by the unjustified attacks upon the Pharisees contained in the New Testament. Rabbi Marmur admires the serene Christian spirituality, but like most of the other writers in this set, he insists that there must be – within monotheism – many ways to God.

I am not sure that the Muslim writer would agree. Insistence upon the Koran as the dictated word of God makes it difficult for him to do much more than quote it at us. And what it says, apparently, is that while Christians are the next best things to Muslims, Jesus was *not* the Son of God – he was just a divinely inspired prophet (peace be upon him) and did not even die on the cross. The Islamic view, of which I must confess I was not aware, is that God himself rescued Jesus from the cross and saved him from his enemies by raising him up to heaven. Islam rejects the doctrines of the crucifixion, we are told, and this rejection is based upon the authority of God himself as revealed in the Koran, and upon a deeper rejection of blood sacrifice and vicarious atonement.

The Hindu contributor complains about the coldness and gloom of Christianity, its insistence upon sinfulness and the need for repentance; also about the pious Christian's insistence on belief in Christ as an act of faith, instead of something to be tested by experience. The writer, Miss Debjani Chatterjee, remarks that while the Muslim will contest Christianity's claim to be monotheistic – on account of the Trinity – that poses no problem to the Hindu. He is quite accustomed to the mystery of unity in multiplicity, of God who is Brahma as creator, Vishnu as preserver and Shiva as destroyer. Hinduism, too, she writes, believes in a gracious God who incarnates himself for the salvation of the world. But whereas Christians insist upon only one incarnation, Hindus believe in many *avatars*, and can accept Jesus as one of them. Miss Chatterjee concludes with a tribute to the example set by Christians in their dedication to social work.

Perhaps most agreeable to Christian ears will be the article by the Sikh contributor, Piara Singh Sambhi, although he does reject the unique divinity of Christ and is particularly shocked by the statues, candles and elaborate paraphernalia of Roman Catholicism. The Quakers, he says, come nearest to Sikh ideals, for Sikhs, like the Society of Friends, have neither sacraments nor clergy. They do not regard the practical and the religious life as independent spheres, and they believe that the Spirit of God is in everyone, so that we are all in that sense divine. Further, Sikhs find it difficult to accept the doctrine of original sin, or the necessity for baptism or rebirth in Christ. And like all the other writers, the Sikh complains of the exclusiveness of Christianity, which he thinks contrasts oddly with the words of Peter, 'God has no favourites, but in every nation the man who is God-fearing and does what is right is acceptable to him.'

Martyrs to R.E.

15 October 1977

There was a piquant juxtaposition of ecclesiastical events the other day: in Westminster Abbey, the unveiling of a memorial to the martyrs (both Protestant and Catholic) of the English Reformation, and just round the corner, the publication by the Church of England's Board of Education of a study of the failure of religious education. There they were, side by side in my diary – faithfulness unto death and bored indifference. And which do we prefer, a tolerance that seems almost to extinguish faith, or a fanaticism that sends men and women to the stake?

There is no question which of my two appointments was the more uplifting. The Abbey service was truly ecumenical, down to the very positioning of the memorial itself at the feet of an inscription to Protestant Elizabeth and Catholic Mary, each of whom had hanged, burned and tortured by the score. Dean Carpenter's superb address dodged none of the contradictions, evaded none of the painful facts: not the atrocities which had disfigured Christendom, not the scandal of violence done by Christian against Christian, nor the near certainty that – had the situation been reversed – many of the martyrs would have been found among the persecutors. Still, they had brought grace and dignity to scenes of squalid barbarity, and they had reminded us in these days of indifference and fleeting fashion that the imperatives of conscience are categorical – that there *is* a difference between the true and the untrue – even though the truth of God must be greater than all our several insights put together.

Religious freedom is now one of the commonplaces of Christendom. We no longer believe in suppressing heresy by burning the heretic, or in saving souls from error by applying the rack. But does this mean that all opinions are equally valid – that when it comes to spiritual matters, there are no authoritative teachings worth pressing with any emphasis?

Apparently that is the impression that religious education has left upon our own young people, if the Church House report *A Kind of Believing* is itself to be believed. Two things in it stand out: the repeated assertion that everything about religion is, to the young, boring – and the insistence that everybody should be left to make up their own mind about what to believe, because it is entirely your own affair. So private an affair, in fact, that the kids can't even talk to themselves about it and have the utmost difficulty in articulating their beliefs to an interviewer.

The reaction of boredom says something, I am afraid, about the poor standards of religious teaching in our schools. But I think it says something also about the meaningfulness of what is taught, and about the kids' deceived obsession with excitement, action, anything but dreary old abstract ideas. The young people in the survey also seem to be addicts of anything dressed up as scientific fact. They reject the Bible because, *you* know, how *could* the Red Sea part – it must all be a fairy story. Yet they eagerly theorize about the reality of flying saucers and poltergeists. Oddly, their 'alternative culture' seems to have left them no values.

I find it all very disturbing indeed. As the report observes, by endorsing the 'privatization' of belief – by agreeing it is everyone's own affair – we are destroying any kind of consensus which might hold society together. If we are never to expose our inner beliefs to our fellows, who knows what dangerous nonsense we may deceive ourselves with? Worse still, our souls may become vacant hollows stuffed with cotton wool.

Do we go back, then, to authoritarian instruction hammering home the literal truths of the rival churches? It is an illusion, surely, to think that we could, let alone should. There are some who argue that if old-style religion is perishing it is only because the Holy Spirit wills it so and has something more appropriate up its sleeve: faith, perhaps, that is lived and seen to be lived, not just celebrated on Sundays in a Gothic cage. And this living of faith is surely how it was always meant to be – the divorce of faith from life is relatively new. But can we live faith without running into martyrdom once more? Or can we save our immortal souls only at the cost of our bodies?

Call me Mother

22 October 1977

Greatly trembling, I take up today the question of women priests. The matter must be taken up again soon by the General Synod of the Church of England; it will certainly be discussed at the Lambeth Conference next summer, after which the Church of England will have to make up its mind if it really means to enact what in principle it has already approved – the ordination of women as priests. Parts of the Anglican Communion have already done so, and the present Archbishop of Canterbury thinks the time has come for England to follow suit. But his predecessor, Lord Ramsey, counsels ecumenical tact – do nothing to upset the Roman Catholic and Orthodox churches. Say the Orthodox, 'Women priests would be an insuperable barrier to unity', and the Romans, 'Though some women may *feel* they have a vocation, the Church, in obedience to its Lord, is not authorized to ordain them.'

It ought to be noted, I think, that the Church of Rome does not even recognize the validity of Anglican *male* priests. However, just as ecumenism is coming to the boil once more, this disruptive – and some would say marginal – issue has been dumped into the pot (so it is claimed) on behalf of an exhibitionist minority. Not my own words, but there they are. And I know that even some sympathizers with the women's cause regard the recent transatlantic commando raid by the Reverend Alison Palmer of Washington D.C. – two quick Eucharists and out – as less than helpful to the cause.

Now I must admit that, being neither Anglican, Orthodox nor Roman Catholic, I have to make a very strenuous effort to see the case against ordaining women. My reaction is to say, 'If they can be doctors, judges and trombonists – why not priests?' But then my own religious society has no priests at all, and I came to it by way of the Free churches which have had women ministers for over seventy years. They, I fancy, must be a trifle miffed at all the fuss being made about not offending the hierarchies of Rome and Istanbul. Yet it is vital to appreciate the fundamental difference between this view of the ministry and the rather older view of the priesthood.

To simplify the latter, a priest is directly descended by laying on of hands from the apostles. His supreme function is to represent Christ at the Eucharist. And since the incarnation chose the form of a man, that representation can only be made in male form. It will not do to say it was human form and that therefore any human form is acceptable. I hope I do not offend when I say there is a powerful element of the magical in this, and I am well aware that it is an element that many people do require, and find, in their religion.

On the other hand, the Free churches hold the apostles to have been unique and without successors, and the priesthood to have been a late and improper intrusion without Scriptural basis. What really matters here is the preaching of the Word. The minister is a teacher, a prophet even, but there is nothing supernatural about him or what he does.

Thus for anyone in the Free Church position, there is hardly any problem in ordaining women. But for those who adhere to the centuries-old traditions of the magical church (and the Church of England manages, as usual, to be a bit of both), the issue is very serious. For to them, authentic and unchanging continuity matters immensely – otherwise the Church would be a mere human invention to be tinkered with ad lib.

There is no time to go through the whole armoury of arguments against the ordination of women. They range from the supposed essential maleness of God the Father (and we are reminded darkly that only pagan fertility cults have priestesses), through the fact that Jesus did choose men only as his apostles, down to some old-fashioned views about the basic natures of men and women – for example, that women are 'too emotional' while men are 'better at abstract ideas'. There are also some rather muffled gynaecological objections, and a certain amount of rather less muffled woman-hating which in some cases could use the help of a psychiatrist. But there is by now a highly organized 'Theology of the Men Only Priesthood'. Anyone who dares to quote 'In Christ there is neither male nor female' is quickly clobbered with I Corinthians 11 and 14.

In this duel there is a riposte to every thrust. Surely Christ was bound to follow the sexual rules of the day? Ah, but he overstepped them constantly in his generosity to women! Then may not the Holy Spirit itself be calling us to ordain them? Ah, but how do we know it is the Holy Spirit and not just a passing fad?

As I say, it is not really my battle. But if Jesus were to come again and were to find women administering the sacraments in his name, do you think he would respond with wrath and sorrow, or with fellowship and love?

Violence in Rhodesia

29 October 1977

There has been a good deal of biting and scratching over a recent pamphlet from the International Affairs Division of the British Council of Churches, entitled *Rhodesia Now*. For 30p, it offers not only a compact history of the various attempts to negotiate a settlement, but also a presentation of the case on violence which I think every Christian would do well to study, if not approve.

At this point, those who regard all councils of churches as conspiracies of pinko priests who ought to keep their noses in their prayer-books, might do well to switch off. Or they might stay to endorse the views of Mr John Page, the Tory M.P., who rang me up to condemn what he saw as the Council's call for unstinting support for terrorists who were murdering women and children. Surely, he demanded, the Church ought always to support peaceful change and reconciliation?

Well, the Council's pamphlet sets out a number of options and does, in fact, say that negotiations are always preferable to conquest and that we should continue to work for that.

The pamphlet also urges that we pray for the sufferers of all races, and seek to understand the great strains under which white people are living in Rhodesia. But there is no question what the Council thinks (and has long thought) should happen in Rhodesia: the transfer of power to a majority-ruled African state in which those whites who want to do so may continue to find a home. It makes no concessions to those who argue that an African state will inevitably become just another black tyranny, or that white paternalism ensures Christian standards of civilization. Africans must be allowed to choose, can't be held back by barrier excuses. As for the 'kith and kin' appeal, to quote the Reverend Arthur MacArthur, Vice-President of the

British Council, 'It is not possible for the Christian to rest on that. Christian brotherhood transcends that kind of relationship.' In other words, it is time to remember that nine-tenths of the Church in Rhodesia is black. And this, in fact, has helped to provide the B.C.C. with a very extensive grass roots intelligence network. It is not guessing at a distance.

And the pamphlet goes on to explain, without at all endorsing everything they do, why African Christians feel justified in resorting to violence. But first it makes one highly realistic point: that following the long failure of sanctions and negotiations, a situation of war does now exist in Rhodesia, so it is of rather limited value to theorize about supporting peaceful change. As a leading Methodist said to me, on his return from visiting Rhodesia, 'The language of war is now taking over both sides.'

And that is what war, what violence, does. Irrespective of the merits of the case, it takes you over and *it* runs *you*. Part of the argument for the Just War is that for the victims of oppression to deny themselves the use of force against a forceful Government is for those victims to allow injustice a walk over. The pacifist has got to start his non-violent resistance very early in the day to avoid that dilemma. But no doubt he will still argue that violence can seldom be controlled to produce the results that its practitioners vow they intend. And it is my impression that there are few, if any, pacifists among the British Council's critics. They would be most welcome. The pamphlet states the pacifist case, but it says that Rhodesia's Christians oblige us to concede that support for violence *is* compatible with *some* expressions of Christian conscience.

What this says to me, though I do not relish it, is that Christians cannot afford to get hung up on the violence of either side. Nor, says the B.C.C., on the fact that Communists help the guerrillas. Some of its officials are rather surprised that the critics do not see that the longer the struggle goes on, the more blacks will be forced into Marxist positions.

Why is it that these British churches, once so staunchly

aligned with Empire, are no longer prepared to say 'Our country – right or wrong'? Realism? Opportunism? Or even something to do with the Gospel? Just to provide the obligatory, self-neutralizing balance to this leftish picture of the B.C.C., let me record the views of the exiled Bishop of Namibia, Colin Winter. He says he finds our churches reactionary, élitist, sycophantic and platitudinous. Just like the good old days, in fact.

Sex and the Synod

12 November 1977

Sex raised its lovely head in the midst of the General Synod of the Church of England this week, and found the Church with a pretty guilty conscience. 'I feel so strongly,' said one clergyman, 'that the Church has in the past too often damaged rather than helped society to cope with sexuality . . .', and he went on to point out that a century ago, when the working people of Britain were being systematically dehumanized by capitalism, the Church was devoting most of its energies to condemning sexual and doctrinal aberrations.

Why is it no longer so preoccupied with these matters? And should we be better off if it were? The Synod had before it two rival resolutions, one calling for a new look at the whole theology of Christian sexuality in the light of the present theological and psychiatric understandings, and the other welcoming the recent Vatican Declaration on Sexual Ethics 'as a necessary and compassionate restatement of traditional Christian teaching in these matters'. (I must say, for myself, I am always a little doubtful when people talk about *Christian* sexuality or the *theology* of sexuality, instead of just plain sexuality, or better still – sex. But let it pass for the moment.)

The debate, to the disappointment of a heavily-reinforced press-gallery, never really caught fire. Perhaps it was a little too early in the morning. But I make no apology for dwelling on the opening address by Canon Rhymes of Southwark, who moved the 'liberal' motion – not because I am backing his case, but because I think it was an intelligent and enlightening analysis of what is in fact going on in sexual ethics.

First, says Canon Rhymes, the Church is moving away at last from the idea that sex is for procreation only. It is now seen as the expression of an emotional and spiritual relationship, and the new marriage service speaks of the delight, tenderness and joy with which husband and wife may 'know each other in love' (a phrase over which there has been some tittering, though not from me). Far more often than not, they make entirely honest love with every intention of *not* conceiving a child.

Furthermore, says Canon Rhymes, we are moving away from rigid rules of gender. It seems clear that the so-called male and female characteristics are not limited to their particular sexes in anything like as narrow a way as we once imagined. But even more important, the advances in scientific knowledge made more than a century ago are only now beginning to filter through to our moral assumptions. Before the invention of the microscope in 1838, it was thought that the male seed by itself was a human being in miniature. (There may have been a few scientifically enlightened souls, but that was the widespread popular instinct.) Adam was the almighty male, copied from God, with the whole human race in his loins. Eve – woman – was a mere seed-bed, an incubator. Hence, from this false understanding derived the severe attitude towards masturbation and 'the sin of Onan', the shame of the barren woman, the superiority of men, the inferiority of women, the vileness of homosexuality (with a short 'o', please) and much else. Only the microscope has revealed that the roles of the sexes are complementary to each other, that humankind is created in perfect equality. And until we have accepted that, says Canon Rhymes, we shall never think straight about sexual ethics. Too much of the Church's teachings on these matters remains rooted in pre-microscopic thinking.

But at last we are moving away from the 'Dirty, Disgusting and Don't' view of sex, the 'Government Health Warning' attitude, into the realization that 'sex is fun and funny' (to quote the Reverend Michael Saward, Evangelical and author of *And So to Bed*). Anglo-Catholics like Father Brian Brindley of Oxford might lament the sexual confusion of our times, but Canon Rhymes got another shot in by observing that dictatorship always seems to embrace puritanical sexuality. Next after bashing the blacks, he claimed, the National Front and their friends put bashing the gays.

And so, with much reference to the works of Dr Jack Dominian (q.v. – he is the Roman Catholic revisionist in these matters), the Church of England is about to launch yet another enquiry. Some might say it was a bourgeois distraction from the evils of capitalism or racism. But I suspect, myself, that sex is the one area still most likely to confront the average man or woman with the dilemma, 'Is this right – or wrong?'

Human Wrongs Day

10 December 1977

It is Human Rights Day, and alarmingly I detect the shadow of a yawn – for it is one of the perils of our time that the media which expose injustice can also over-expose it. People begin to ask themselves what they can possibly do about it all and whether there isn't a touch of exaggeration there anyway. Also, one man's right is another man's treason. Our hearts bleed for Soviet dissidents, but Communist subversives deserve everything they get. There is also that argument about not interfering in other countries' internal affairs. If we insist upon doing that, we really must not object to their returning the compliment. Personally I think it would be no bad thing if they did. It would help to keep us morally on our toes.

At the same time, it is up to those who do campaign for human rights to do so intelligently, even with some cunning.

I would not care to be dogmatic about whether more good is done by embarrassing oppressive regimes in public or by confronting them in private. Both are probably necessary in judicious proportions. In either case, though, we have to discern the difference between demanding that human beings be treated as human beings, and demanding that (say) a Communist regime treat them as if it were a democracy.

How frightened human beings have become of one another's ideas! We must be extremely uncertain of the love of God protecting us. It is commonplace to say that we live in an age when the use of torture to suppress human rights is more widespread than ever. I am not entirely sure that this is true. Our Lord was the victim of a hideous torment that was extremely widespread – and public – in the ancient world. But I suppose the methods now available – the drugs, electric shocks and sensory deprivation – may be subtler. It is not so easy nowadays to *die* under torture. But surely the example of our Lord is a very good reason why the suffering of anyone – even (should I say?) an Asian or a Semite – should concern us all.

There are good theological grounds for concern over human rights. If we are made in God's image – if we are made by God at all – then any attempt to violate or degrade that image is blasphemy. God has a claim, it is argued, upon the human being as he made him, and it is part of our stewardship of creation to care for one another as he designed us. And, to quote the Archbishop of Canterbury, we are not permitted to take a narrow view of who is our kith and kin.

Religion very properly tends to emphasize duties rather than rights – and rights are the other side of duties. But different societies elevate different rights. The Anglo-Saxon countries today (mindful of past Fascism) tend to emphasize the individual's rights over the State. Socialist countries tend to put things the other way round, in the supposed interests of the workers. And in the Third World you hear much of the rights of races and peoples, as against more powerful peoples and races.

In the past the Church itself has not had a blameless record as a champion of human rights – though it may be said to be making up for lost time now. You may think here that I am referring to its support for African guerrilla movements, though in fact I had Latin America in mind. Anywhere our motives are always mixed and it would be hard to clear the churches entirely of the charge of opportunism, of having a certain instinct for the winning side.

One Rhodesian acquaintance of mine complains that 'the missionaries spend too much time with the blacks and are totally out of touch with the ordinary white man'. Still, it just is not so (as he claims) that the churches never criticize the Communists and only denounce the excesses of the whites. The work of organizations like Keston College, Centre for the Study of Religion and Communism, or Amnesty International, says otherwise. Yet it is indeed true that church leaders like Bishop Huddleston do sincerely believe that racism is a greater curse than Communism. And if they do lecture their white kith and kin rather than the guerrillas, it is probably because one has a certain right to lecture one's relatives, one's fellow Christians. If you want to influence strangers, you have to proceed more circumspectly.

In the end, the point about human rights is that they are the only way to defeat their opposite – human oppression. And the terrible thing about oppression is that it destroys the humanity of *both* sides – the torturer as well as the tortured, the security man as well as the guerrilla. Our prayers must be for both.

Faith and Figures

17 December 1977

One of the drawbacks about being a journalist in religious affairs is that there are so many opinions and so few facts. Everyone wants to comment, but what are they really talking about?

So, full marks to the Evangelical Alliance for producing Volume 2 of its *U.K. Protestant Missions Handbook 1978* – price £1 – and to the Central Statistical Office for its booklet *Sources of Statistics on Religion*. Both, in fact, are edited by the same man, Government statistician John Brierly, to whom students of religion in Britain are much indebted. The *Handbook* also includes an interpretative article by Tom Houston, Executive Director of the Bible Society.

Even if, between them, these booklets can't give you all the answers you may want, at least they tell you where to enquire for them. For example, if you are puzzled that there is only an *estimate* of 19,000 Christian Scientists in Britain, you can find the telephone number to call for an explanation of why Christian Science is opposed to numbering the faithful. You can also find out how to get in touch with such exotics as the Chinese church in London, the Countess of Huntingdon's Connection, the Darby Brethren and the Theosophical Society.

At first sight, however, the general effect is a depressing one and there is no use pretending otherwise. As Tom Houston puts it: 'The picture in the larger denominations is one of unabated decline of a very serious nature.' The Church of England, for example, is shrinking at a rate which would halve its membership before the end of the century. Today (which, to be accurate, means the research done in 1975), of every 1,000 adults in Britain only 182 attend church on an average Sunday. Somewhat better than used to be assumed, perhaps, but compare it with the finding that of every 1,000 adults and children, 680 claim to be Christians – 491 of them Church of England. How come there are so many more Christians around than actually go to church? Is it just that they are lazy – or that the churches are not giving them what they need?

I find it intensely interesting that the more talk there is of Christian unity, the more ecumenical visiting and conferring, the more the denominations seem to proliferate, the more splinter-sects and house-churches seem to multiply, breaking bread together in extra-canonical ways. You might have thought that with the Christian pilgrims surrounded by Red Indian pagans, they would come together more. But the Indians are not actually aggressive, they are indifferent, and the pilgrims are breaking up into little clusters, each making its own way to the promised land.

Talking of Indians, it is the Hindus, Muslims and Buddhists and Sikhs who are on the up and up these days. Tom Houston says, 'Britain is not only becoming *less* Christian because of declining faith among former adherents – it is increasingly *anti*christian because of the rise of other faiths,' and he adds, 'We should not delude ourselves that it is purely from immigration, or assume that in time it will be absorbed.'

I cannot myself endorse the term *anti*christian, though some of the literature distributed by the heretical Ahmadiya Muslim sect is provocative, to say the least. And I have my doubts about how many English people are actually converting to Buddhism or even that rather attractive form of Protestant Hinduism, Sikhism.

The black churches are on the increase, as the black British turn to them for the sense of identity and joy that they are not likely to find in many of our own churches. But so far as white people are concerned, those churches which are pulling in the new recruits (though scarcely on a very large scale) are the so-called Christian deviations – the Jehovah's Witnesses, Mormons, Spiritualists (perhaps a symptom of the loneliness of our old people), certain Evangelical Fundamentalists, and the Reverend Ian Paisley's Free Presbyterians. There is much American influence among these. At a time when the old-established churches are becoming more flexible, less exclusive, people seem to be looking for close-knit certainties.

Tom Houston thinks the churches are victims of pessimism, that they should think of growth in terms of quality and not just quantity, and that they are splendidly equipped now to take the offensive. Well, maybe. It would be nice to think so, with all my heart. But could such an offensive as the churches are likely to contemplate capture the vast army not of sectarians but of spiritual free-lances?

Festival of Fathers

24 December 1977

About a year ago, just before I started doing these talks, I had the following letter from an elderly listener, a lady it turned out, living in Bristol.

Dear Gerald Priestland (it said),

I am sure you will be taking part in the Christmas-time broadcasts, so forgive my suggesting an unusual point. A week or so back, the Archbishop of York did a series of talks emphasizing the *fatherhood* of God. Now, my father was a stern Victorian, and we were scared stiff of him. Fear came first, respect, admiration and affection in lesser degree after. My gentle mother taught us that God was like 'a great big Father' (as she put it). My life-size father being more than I could stand, a great big Father in heaven was the last straw.

Ours was a religious home, and I learned my prayers as soon as I could babble. But, as a growing child, seeing the incoming tides, the sunset, flowers growing in fields, kittens and so forth, I got to starting the Lord's Prayer 'creator in heaven' – and in my middle eighties I still do.

Some fifty years ago, a group of us opened a club in a very bad slum behind the cathedral here in Bristol. I had boys of between thirteen and sixteen in my Sunday class. We always ended the session with the Lord's Prayer, and looking round the circle of bent heads I wondered what on Earth it could convey to them. They had fathers not at home but in prison. Four or five had drunken fathers. And there were two wizened little brothers who were sent into the market every Saturday to pinch a couple of rabbits for Sunday dinner. They were punished severely if they came back empty-handed. So I moved my class into the mornings and got them into the country. They had never seen wild roses or violets actually growing, or clouds chasing over a long space of sky, or an incoming tide. I tried to show God as creator, and now after more than fifty years, think that the best way.

The letter continues:

How little we know of the holy family! But the eldest son usually followed his father's trade. So from the age of twelve, Jesus and Joseph must have spent hours every day in each other's company. The relationship between them must have been of a very high order. For, years later, when the young preacher wanted a strong, tender word with which to express the relationship of God to us, he chose the word 'Father'. Why have we neglected this good old man, Joseph? Do give a word if you can and bring him out of the shadows.

And that was the end of this moving letter from a woman who had clearly longed to love her father, and with that longing projected (for me, at any rate) a new warmth into the personality of St Joseph.

It has been my object, in reading that letter, to present Christmas not just as a children's feast, nor even a day on which to honour the motherhood of Mary, but as our Father's day – a day on which children might seek to honour their fathers with love, while fathers look deep into their hearts and ask themselves (and I think this is the real challenge of that letter from Bristol) 'Have I deserved the love of my child – or only his dread and fear? Had Jesus been *my* son, would he have used *my* title as a synonym for the God of love?'

One aspect of Christmas that's too often missed is the awesome trust that is laid upon fathers and mothers the world over. 'Whoso shall offend one of these little ones which believe in me, it were better for him that a millstone were hanged about his neck, and that he were drowned in the depth of the sea.' How's that for a Christmas card inscription? Perhaps on behalf of one of the organizations caring for battered wives and children. There is little doubt that the best way to produce violent children is not to set them watching violent television, but to leave them at the mercy of a violent father, whose name they will grow up to revile. One of the marvels of Christmas is that even the Son of God was once at the mercy of a human father. And if my Bristol friend is right, he – Joseph – did not fail his trust. We owe St Joseph a lot.

(Postscript: I have since learned that the writer of the letter is now dead. May she and her father rest together in peace.)

Yours Faithfully

31 December 1977

I've almost completed a year of doing these talks, and I'm happy to say plans are afoot to publish them eventually.

Broadcasting is a strangely lonely business: here one sits in a cupboard with no view, talking to a little wire basket, and wondering if there really *is* anybody out there. Well, the stimulating thing about this job is that – unlike any other I've done during some thirty years in broadcasting – there is so much evidence that people *are* there, some enthusiastic, some hostile, some critical – but none indifferent. The last time I did a booklist 550 people wrote in for it. And that's how it should be – broadcasters should not be allowed one-way communication only, and I think the fact that they appear to claim it, helps to account for some of the resentment they meet.

Though I must say at once that the great majority of my letters are kind and encouraging. I shan't indulge myself to the extent of quoting from them. I'll just say that they are the real reward for doing the job. You don't hesitate to correct my errors and omissions – which are often howling – but you mostly do it tactfully. And I have some very learned, distinguished and reverend correspondents.

One of them, from an Essex rectory, sends me copies of his experimental service for Post-Darwinians – with a Lord's

Prayer that begins, 'Our fatherly creator of time and energy, recognized be thy harmonious power . . .' Quite my favourite, however, is a charming orientalist. I had mentioned that Muslim ladies could obtain a divorce on the grounds of 'unannounced journeyings' by their husbands. Very true, said my correspondent, and he knew a Persian M.P.'s wife who had often contemplated availing herself of it. But, he continued, she had taken her revenge instead by selling huge crates of dates meant for winning votes in the constituency, and used the proceeds to buy shoes. That's one of the gems of my collection.

But not so gem-like are some of the letters that always turn up when I mention race relations or Rhodesia. For example, a Mr A. of Peterborough writes: 'Your programmes now out-Goebbel Goebbels and certainly copy Hitler and Stalin's racist themes. Coloureds have never done anything much for themselves – any progress they've made they owe to the whites.' Well, not to Mr A., I'm sure. Incidentally, obscene and anonymous letters are filtered out by my long-suffering secretary.

There was an outburst of righteous indignation some months ago when (during a discussion of corruption in business) I confessed to having speeded up a reluctant Turkish telephone operator by (shall we say?) tipping her in advance. 'You corrupted the lady by giving her a bribe to do her duty!' pronounced the Reverend C. of south-west London; and Mr R. of Northants observed, 'You will presumably transfer your custom to another hotel.' After making an investment like that? He must be joking!

Much heat was also generated by my indulgence of a slim volume entitled *The Myth of God Incarnate*. Mrs T. of south-east London intoned: 'By making known Satan's writings, you give it power to do its destructive work . . . Satan has already had a good say in the re-translation of the Bible . . .' I was afraid I was in for one of those comminations that usually come on ruled paper, in block capitals and multicoloured ink, but it turned out what was really troubling Mrs T. was *hunting parsons*. She cited forty-two biblical texts and then moved on to one of the lesser-known apocryphal gospels 'not censored by the apostles' as she put it. These are becoming increasingly popular, I find. And, of course, there is my mathematical correspondent who counts his way backwards and forwards through the Bible, proving the immense significance of the number thirty-one.

I am moved, and not a little worried, by the number of people who write asking for help or advice: for I am *not* a priest, and no sort of guru. Sooner or later I am bound to say something you're going to dislike. My deepest respect goes to the half-dozen people who have written stiff letters of complaint, had a stiff note from me in return, and then written back to apologize. But I do drop some clangers. Once I described how people tended to treat a Religious Affairs Correspondent as if he'd had a sex change operation. Two days later: 'Dear Sir – as one about to have a sex change operation . . .' Oh, dear . . .

We and They Make Us

7 January 1978

Anyone who doubts the relevance of religion to what is strangely opposed to it as 'real life' should contemplate the past week. They might begin with the Archbishop of Canterbury warning the Farmington Trust of the folly of expecting the average religious education teacher to conduct a course in comparative religion, and then proceed to Mr Gordon Gorrie, of the Assistant Masters' Association, accusing parents of hypocrisy in requiring teachers to implant in their children religious attitudes and standards which were blatantly flouted by the parents at home. Finally, one might contemplate the Church of England's latest report on the role of imprisonment in our system of law and order. The link between this and Mr Gorrie's remarks is stronger than you might think: once again, it is a matter of the public requiring an institution to enforce standards which the public itself ought to be implanting, in church or in the home.

I must particularly commend the report *Prisons and Prisoners in England Today*, which the Church Information Office has published. It is thoughtfully produced by a group of named and qualified experts and deserves the study of every conscientious congregation. It takes the trouble to point out one excellent biblical reason for Christians to concern themselves with prison: that while the law of Old Testament Israel made ample provision for punishment, it regarded imprisonment as irregular – one of the features of the reign of the Messiah was 'to set the captive free'. Visiting the prisoner was a particular expression of early Christian solidarity with all men – regardless of the reasons for their imprisonment.

Far from being a piece of sloppy do-goodism, the report acknowledges the need for punishment, both for practical and moral reasons. In some cases at least, society really has to be protected by removing the offender from the community. And one cannot ignore the public demand for retribution, however irrational and ill-informed it may often be. The authors of the report then indulge in a fascinating flirtation with this concept of 'retribution', saying that on the one hand it reflects and respects the moral responsibility of the offender but that on the other hand it fails to take account of the fact that moral responsibility is not the same as criminal responsibility – it is something that develops at different rates in different people. Punishment may convey the legitimate disapproval of society, but it ought to do so in a way that does not prevent the moral development of the offender. Since moral growth requires a certain amount of freedom, and since imprisonment deprives the offender of his liberty, the use of imprisonment ought to be kept to the minimum consistent with the need to protect society.

The report believes that imprisonment creates at least as many problems as it solves, and runs a grave risk of destroying or corrupting those entrusted to it. 'Such evidence as there is' (it observes) 'points to the conclusion that group attitudes and the likelihood of detection are more effective than punishment itself in deterring people from committing offences to which they might be inclined.' Since detection is greatly dependent upon public co-operation, what we are being told is that the public – through its own neglect as parent and citizen – gets the crime rate, as well as the immorality, it deserves.

Where the Christian approach stands out is in the report's refusal to see the offender as a different sort of human being set over against an orderly society. There's a splendid quotation here from Bertrand Russell: 'We never feel so good as when we are punishing someone.' Well, we shouldn't: we are all united in sin. We the community differ very little from they the offenders, and we have to show our solidarity with them by caring for them ourselves – not just by handing them over to a prison service which we seldom bother to understand properly, and which we are constantly setting impossible tasks. And the very same is true of our schools. Surely, the Archbishop got it right when he brought it all back to that unfashionable thing, the family. What can be done to restore this neglected, discredited unit?

The Theology of Animals

14 January 1978

In an effort to get these talks off the socio-political track they've got set in recently, I thought I would take a look at the theology of animals – though I'm well aware it will be no light relief for me. I doubt if there's any subject more calculated to get listeners reaching for their pens and typewriters than one that involves such risky trigger-words as vivisection, factory-farming, vegetarianism and dog mess in the streets.

Perhaps I'd better start by declaring my interests. I live

in a city suburb and own a dog and two cats. In the country, one of my daughters keeps a horse. I'm not opposed to fox-hunting (though I don't urge it upon anyone), I eat meat if I can afford it, and I have a scientist son-in-law whose researches into the nerve-chemistry of pain killing promise to be of immense benefit to man *and* beast, and would be quite impossible without the use of laboratory animals – which he does not (in any sense true to our language) 'torture'.

In short, I suspect I am a fairly average person – I certainly feel like one – and although I do not believe one should dodge doing what is morally right simply because 'most people won't do it', I do think one risks becoming rather remote and futile if one starts indulging in moral luxuries. I'm trying to put this kindly, and with the greatest respect for the many sincere champions of animal welfare and vegetarianism. I hope they will not parody my intentions by writing that I'm in favour of raising calves in crates or giving beagles lung cancer. These good friends may be finding the way of the future for us, but they aren't an awful lot of help to those of us who have to cope with everyday life here and now, or to those who have to feed us and heal us. I'm beginning to think the only way to keep one's moral score-card clean is to retire to the B.B.C.'s Iron Age village. But is that, in fact, the life that God has called us to?

I haven't got far with the theology of animals, have I? It's a subject which has produced at least three highly reputable books of late: Andrew Linzey's *Animal Rights*, Peter Singer's *Animal Liberation* and Stephen Clark's *The Moral Status of Animals*. The argument about them seems to turn largely on whether you consider man has been given carnivorous mastery over all other creatures, to use them for his own benefit; or whether man himself is just another animal, and not necessarily a meat-eating one, who must take special pains to respect his fellow creatures in a complex interdependent system. Biblically, I suppose the first three chapters of Genesis *are* vegetarian. Meat-eating comes only after the fall; though the Lord God of the rest of the Old Testament rather fancies meat. As for Jesus, there's no reason to suppose he wasn't a meat-eater, and he seems to have been particularly fond of fish. I really can't believe he would have made a major issue of this, or of alcohol: by most accounts dietary rules did not mean a lot to him.

But, of course, we aren't living in the same world, with the same type of agriculture or the same pressures of population. In a sense, the animals we've raised – the battery hens, the dairy herds – are much more *our* responsibility, though that doesn't imply we can exploit them anyhow we like. Our cruelty degrades us as well as them. Yet I can't help feeling that the thin streak of cruelty in, say, hunting, is somehow true to life: that it's unhealthy to try to rewrite nature altogether.

I haven't, I'm afraid, much patience with colleagues who publish long articles citing figures for tons of dirt and gallons of urine, nasty diseases and fortunes spent on whale meat as sufficient reason for banishing pet dogs from our cities. Yes, they should be more strictly licensed and controlled – or perhaps their owners should, for a bad dog is no more than an ill-trained dog. But the dogs are there *because* of the cities – because the life we have to lead in them is so unnatural we desperately need these scraps of nature to keep us sane, to teach our children about birth and death and dependence and spontaneity – to fill or bridge so many yawning gaps in our way of life – and, above all, to enable us (who often find it so difficult) to *give* love. I didn't mean to get back to the subject of the family again, yet to so many old people who have lost their family, a dog or some other pet is their only opportunity to love. If God loves the sparrow, may not an old man love a budgerigar, or better still, a basset that'll take him for walks?

O Jerusalem

21 January 1978

Jerusalem, says Mr Menachem Begin, shall remain united – the capital city of Israel and of the Jewish people for ever and ever. On the contrary, says President Sadat, it must return to the Arabs from whom it was seized by force. Somewhere in the background, the Christian churches make occasional suggestions about turning the place into an internationalized holy city. But, as they say, how many divisions has the Pope? It will take more than piety to sort this out.

By its very name, Jerusalem *should* be a city of peace. And yet I cannot think of another so bloodstained and ravaged by war – from its destruction by Titus in the first century A.D. to its battering in successive Arab-Israel conflicts over the past thirty years. I have heard it argued by both sides that much of its later agony could have been avoided if the British had phased out the Palestine mandate rather than dropping it and running – easy enough to say if you overlook how the situation actually was, and how fed up most British people then were with the whole affair. But a historian might very well see it as the collapse of the last of a long and disastrous series of Christian crusades – a series that began with Peter the Hermit in 1095, and ended with Allenby evicting the Turks in 1917.

It is a far from noble history – what Christendom has done to Jerusalem, and any pilgrim who goes there should do penance for that as much as for any personal sins. Nowhere has Christian anti-Semitism been more viciously displayed – and nowhere have the Jews hit back more sharply when opportunity presented itself, allying themselves frequently with the later Muslim invaders from whom (by and large) the Jews of Jerusalem got a much better deal than they did from the Christians. Come to that, the Christians themselves were not at all badly treated by their Muslim overlords (in between Crusades). 'They are just and do us no wrong nor show us any violence,' wrote the Patriarch of Jerusalem to a ninth-century colleague in Constantinople. Indeed, there's a case to be made – which I wouldn't want to push into the present-day context – that post-Roman Jerusalem was never happier than when Islam was keeping both Jews and Christians in order.

I can detect, I'm sure, a restless stirring in the Zionist lobby, and it should hardly be necessary to explain to any Bible-reading person just what it was Mr Begin was talking about when he almost choked over the notion of handing back east Jerusalem – the old city. For the Old Testament is one long Jewish love-story about Jerusalem, and much of the New Testament story is rooted in that same romance. Jesus wept over Jerusalem and had to die there precisely because he was a Jew as well – if a heretical one.

And to Muslims, too, this is a holy city. When the Caliph Omar captured it in the year 638 and rode his camel to the site of the Temple, what he had come to see was the spot from which his friend Muhammad had risen to heaven – founder of a faith in which it is possible to trace the simplified essence of both Judaism and Monophysite Christianity. There is something to be said, then, for Jerusalem as a cross-breeding-ground of faith, and one could indulge in erudite theological fantasies of what might have happened if Christianity had not developed in other more Hellenized centres.

The fact is, though, that Christianity was reimported to Jerusalem from elsewhere long after its founder's death. The city we see today is nothing like the city he knew – the sites are dubious, the shrines debatable, and the churches that worship him (one ventures to doubt) not quite what he had in mind. Even so, with the clear light falling on the honey-coloured stone and the scent of pine and pepper-vines, it remains a most magical city, standing not just for God's holiness, but for our martyrdom and blasphemy of him for ever. Christians should remind themselves, I suppose, that 'He is not here – he is risen', but they should still, I think, pray for the peace of Jerusalem.

Intercommunion or Bust

28 January 1978

Perhaps you need to be a religion addict to recognize it, but Dr Coggan's address in Westminster Roman Catholic Cathedral the other day was nothing short of sensational – and that for several reasons, not the least of which was that he said it all in the presence (and indeed with the co-operation) of Cardinal Hume. But perhaps I had better recall, to begin with, what the Archbishop *did* say.

The service was part of the recent week of prayer for Christian unity, and Dr Coggan complained about the slow progress which had been made (despite the apostolic exhortation, *Evangelii Nuntiandi*) in joint evangelistic work – especially (as the Archbishop remarked) 'in view of the speed with which forces inimical to Christianity press on with their programmes'. He went on to wonder out loud whether the feebleness of the Christian impact upon the world could be traced to the fact (and here I resume direct quotation) 'that we are divided at the deepest point of unity, the sacrament of the body and blood of Christ? Is this God's judgement on us for failing to grasp this nettle? We recognize our unity in baptism, we persist in disunity at the Eucharist.'

A few moments later, the Archbishop was repeating very much what he said in Rome last April: 'Throughout the world, men and women, ordained and lay, in both our Communions, are refusing to continue in disunity, in what Christ intended to be the sacrament of unity – Roman Catholics receiving at Anglican hands the tokens of Christ's passion and vice versa. Order within the Church matters, and encouragement must not be given to the breaking of rules. But I ask, is the Holy Spirit speaking to the leadership of our churches through the voice of people who see, with a charity sometimes hidden from our eyes, the scandal of disunity?'

Dr Coggan made it clear that he had shown his address in advance to Cardinal Hume and that 'He has expressed himself happy that I should say it, even though he is unable to agree with me because of theological differences'. Let's hope the Cardinal will respond frankly about those differences when he addresses the General Synod of the Church of England next week. However, the statement that he was 'happy' to let the Archbishop speak as he did will only confirm the fear among conservative Roman Catholics that (as Ronald Butt wrote in *The Times* in another context) 'It is precisely to this sort of left-wing view that the Cardinal listens these days and by which he is largely influenced'.

Dr Coggan, we're always told, is a man in a hurry. He has not long to go before retirement, and it's tempting to see his call to intercommunion as an impatient attempt to brush past the hierarchy and incite the faithful to mutiny. For in spite of his talk of not wanting indiscipline, that is precisely how it must seem in Rome. The Vatican keeps saying that sharing the Eucharist can only come as the consummation of reunion – it cannot be exploited as a step *towards* it, and it is very hard to see how it can be otherwise if you accept the Roman view of the Church. It all depends on what you think you are doing at the Eucharist – and how much you care what your neighbour at the altar rail thinks *he* is doing. It is very hard to see how one can reconcile numbers 28, 30 and 31 of the Thirty-nine Articles with Roman theory and practice since the Council of Trent. The 1971 Anglican-Roman Catholic statement steered delicately around questions like transubstantiation and sacrifice, but it left unresolved such matters as reservation, Communion in both kinds, and the whole (surely basic) question of the validity of Anglican orders.

There are, I know, many Christians – including some Roman Catholics – who think these matters are a load of tedious, archaic rubbish which must send God's angels screaming up the wall. But I'm prepared to bet there are many others who take them very seriously indeed, and who would no more think of giving up the centuries-old traditions of their church than they would of giving away part of their country. I personally find it enormously thrilling to hear the Archbishop suggest that the Holy Spirit is calling us to shared Communion – just as he suggested it might be calling to the ordination of women. But who can claim to speak for the Spirit?

Cardinal Points

4 February 1978

Last week, the Archbishop of Canterbury in Roman Catholic company, urging the legalization of shared Communion. This week, the Cardinal Archbishop of Westminster, before the General Synod in Church House, making his response.

In the sense of being the first of its kind, the Cardinal's address did indeed make history. But in doctrinal terms it did no such thing, and nobody who appreciates the nature and speed of the Church of Rome should have thought that it would or could have made history. Cardinal Hume declared that he was speaking in his own name and not as an emissary of the Holy See; and indeed he made his own heartache over the division of Christianity an extremely personal pain, but there was nothing else anywhere in his address which could not be traced back to some recent Vatican document. Perhaps the most interesting question still remains the one raised last week: did Archbishop Coggan really expect anything else?

With his vibrant voice, white hair and black monk's habit, the Cardinal is a figure of such presence that he could read out the calendar of saints for half an hour and still have held his audience in rapt attention – which is not to say that he did anything so meaningless in content. I venture to suggest, however, that it was not until he was half way through his text that he began to do rather more than register fairly standard concerns about the world – race relations, political extremism, pornography, arms spending. And then he turned to the work of the Anglican/Roman

Catholic International Commission, reminding the Synod that neither church had so far formally ratified the Commission's three agreed statements on the Eucharist, ministry and authority. Indicating a wide acreage of theological work still ahead, the Cardinal suggested that issues about the Eucharist and the ordained ministry could not be resolved until there was agreement on the whole nature of the Church, and upon what differences of doctrinal emphasis or practice could be allowed within it. A strong hint followed to proceed no further with the ordination of women in the Anglican Communion. And the special role of the Pope – based upon the Petrine texts – was reaffirmed.

The Cardinal concluded his address on a positive note, urging local churches of all denominations to collaborate wherever they could. But before that, he explained in traditional terms why intercommunion could not be sanctioned. 'We believe,' he said, 'that this sharing presupposes not only the same belief in the reality of Christ's presence . . . but also a common faith in general. I do not question for one moment that the desire of so many to share the same Eucharist is anything but a gift from God . . . But we recognize that there are other questions to be resolved before we can, as Churches, approach the altar of the Lord together.'

That might, perhaps, be interpreted as leaving a loophole for Anglicans and Catholics as individuals to share Communion (though the loophole is a narrow one), but imprecision is not a characteristic of the Church of Rome in these matters, even if it is in the Church of England. Already voices are to be heard, and letters to be read in *The Times*, accusing Dr Coggan of speaking too much for himself and in too emotional a tone of voice. In particular, it is asked, just *how* widespread is the distress caused by the inability of Anglicans and Roman Catholics to take Communion together – or, looked at another way, how widespread is this illicit intercommunion? Most Anglicans and Romans seem perfectly happy following their own rites – very few want or need to cross over (or so it is argued) – I don't know how it can be measured. But whether there would be more Christians in a united church than in the two separate ones seems at least debatable.

A letter from the Roman Catholic Chaplain to the University of York went on to suggest that it was time the two churches drew apart a bit and pulled themselves together. The progress made by the International Commission had been largely offset, wrote the Chaplain, by Anglican academics playing fast and loose with the incarnation and the resurrection. Lay that alongside the Cardinal's address, and I would say it spelt 'hasten slowly'. And yet even the Cardinal speaks of the urgent need for a clear, prophetic voice.

Work or What?

11 February 1978

I have to spend a good deal of my time attending church conferences, and I'm glad to say that nowadays they are increasingly realistic about the problems of everyday life.

The British Council of Churches and several of its constituent members have debated and put out reports on questions like racism, crime and punishment, pornography, and – recently – unemployment. The General Synod of the Church of England was debating that earlier this month in terms which could well have enlightened the House of Commons (which is actually just across the road).

For a start, the Church isn't nearly as optimistic about the chances of Britain getting back to full employment as the Government or the opposition. The first thing we've got to do, it seems, is face the fact that permanent, built-in unemployment is emerging as part of the structure of most economically advanced countries. We don't realize how fast technological advance is abolishing jobs nor how fast people are moving out of manufacture into the service industries, nor the considerable increase in the labour supply that lies ahead – especially as more and more women go out looking for jobs. The dangerous frustration of thousands of young school-leavers who can't even get started on their working careers is already proving a nightmare.

Before I go any further, I had better assure any overseas listeners that the British churches are very well aware that conditions are even worse in the Third World. In general, about 5 per cent of the labour force is un- or under-employed in the West: in the developing countries it is about 35 per cent. And, says the Church, with only 7 per cent of the world's output coming from the Third World – which is making a modest demand to be allowed 25 per cent – the West cannot, dare not, try to solve its problems by denying a new economic order.

In any case, the old ideas that more investment leads to more jobs, and that harder work leads to more wealth, simply aren't as true as they once were, and countries like Britain have got to revise the old Protestant work ethic, which taught the immorality of idleness. In its day it was the inspiration of British (and still more, American) business and empire-building. And it led the ordinary man to find his whole significance in his work. What are you? And the answer is, 'I'm a shipbuilder, a miner, a journalist'. If the changing economic system is going to take away the platform of work on which a man stands, then we have got to find some alternative for him.

Of course, one way about it is to try and spread the work – by shortening the working week, by giving longer holidays, sabbaticals, lowering the age of retirement, and by cutting out the overtime that so many factory workers have come to expect. Or, say the churches, we could reorganize production into smaller units, workers' co-operatives, village workshops. What nobody dares quite suggest is that women be told to stay at home and stick to the children and the kitchen. But to do that, surely, is barely worse than throwing somebody on the scrap-heap of retirement at – when? Sixty? Fifty-five? Fifty? Is it going to be an *offence* to work – and if so, what about writers, artists and composers? And, quite apart from anything else, how are we going to pay our way while working less? We assume, I suppose, that the machines and/or North Sea oil are going to take care of that (though my own Protestant conscience is very uneasy about it). But either way – unemployed or partly employed – the British will have to decide what to do with the extra time on their hands. It's a great opportunity for religion and real study. My time in Asia has convinced me that the sheer busyness of the Anglo-Saxons is a great enemy of spiritual depth. And it is also an enemy of family life and the nurture of children. One of the lessons the British have to learn from Asia and Africa is family solidarity. It still exists among our Hindu, Sikh and Muslim immigrants, and I pray that we don't destroy it. With more time to spare we might even imitate it.

The Bunyan Pilgrimage

18 February 1978

This year, many writers and broadcasters will be paying homage to the memory of Sir Thomas More – born 500 years ago to become truly a saint for all Christians, Catholics and Protestants alike, and for all who would maintain (in More's own words), 'That in things touching conscience, every true and good subject is more bound to have respect to his said conscience and to his soul than to any other thing in all the world beside.'

Among those who would surely have said 'Amen' to that was the man whom I prefer to celebrate today – John Bunyan, of *Pilgrim's Progress*, which was published 300 years ago this month. And I prefer to celebrate Bunyan not just out of a desire to be different – and, I must admit, a certain awe of Sir Thomas – but because I really do think Bunyan upheld in his pilgrimage that same banner of conscience that was raised by the Tudor saint.

It's easier, perhaps, to feel at home with the humble pilgrim, and I must admit I have a more material reason for dwelling on him. Unlike Air and Motoring and Travel correspondents, very few free rides come the way of a

Religious Affairs reporter – but I did get one the other day (courtesy of the English Tourist Board and North Bedfordshire Borough Council) to the Bunyan country, around Bedford. After all, why shouldn't Bunyan be able to do for Bedford what Shakespeare has done for Stratford – one being scarcely less famous than the other, at least among foreign visitors? And I must admit, as one who had never been there before, that Bedford is no mean city – with its splendid embankment along the river-side, and its devotion to that noble dish, the Bedfordshire Bacon Clanger, served with bubble and squeak.

It is, however, a city of many newcomers (including a large Italian colony), and – I am informed – a woeful ignorance of its famous son. My information comes from the Reverend Glyn Evans, minister of the Bunyan Meeting-house and spokesman for this year's many festivities. Frankly, he says, the average American or Fijian who sets course for Bedford is likely – by that very intention – to be better informed about Bunyan than the average Bedfordian seems to be. So if the tercentenary gets something across to the natives (let alone the tourists) it'll be well worth while.

After we'd eaten our Clanger, we did the rounds: the village of Elstow, where Bunyan renounced the sins of morris dancing, bell ringing and playing tip-cat; the Hill Difficulty, up which Bunyan lugged his tinker's anvil to the House Beautiful – a house now reduced to a sad ruin; the site of the jail in which he burnt up twelve years of his prime. But – Bedfordshire farming being among the finest in the land – practically nowhere that still qualifies as the Slough of Despond.

Pilgrim's Progress is so much a tale of figures in a landscape that you get quite carried away by the game of reconstructing it all. The grass-rootedness of it, the way every name instantly defines character, and the strenuous truth of this concept of life as a pilgrimage seem to have a universal appeal, even in translation. And it had a happy ending in real life, for within a year of its publication it had become a world-wide best seller, and after all his persecutions and hardships, its author was at liberty, loved, content and famous.

The church, or meeting, of which he was pastor – and which supported him and his family during his long imprisonment – still exists, and to my mind is almost as fine a monument to him as his book. (Though, true to Bunyan's spirit, I think, Mr Evans is wary lest people come there to worship Bunyan rather than God.) On his deathbed, Bunyan insisted that the sacraments must not be a cause of division among Christians, and that (in particular) the mode of baptism – whether by sprinkling of infants or total immersion of believers – should not be a bolt or bar to the Lord's Table. And so, for 300 years, the Bunyan Meeting-house has shown a tolerance rare among Dissenters: today it is affiliated both to the Baptist Union *and* to the Congregational Church – Glyn Evans himself being United Reformed. In my last two talks in this series I have been at some pains to explain why many Christians attach so much importance to forms and doctrines. In Bedford it is not only Protestants who may be refreshed by the reminder of another way; up the Hill Difficulty through the Valley of Humiliation, following the star of Conscience.

Facing the Front

25 February 1978

There's a cartoon of Adolf Hitler marching through a forest of swastika'd banners and upraised arms. Out of the forest floats a small caption, reading: 'I don't agree with what he says, but I'll defend to the death his right to say it . . .'

Should democracy allow totalitarians the liberty to destroy freedom? And should the Church concede to political extremists the right to assault Christian values? For whether or not you believe the churches should 'interfere' in political matters, those extremists (from either end) would not hesitate to intervene drastically in religious concerns if *they* came to power. Particularly, I fancy, those who bitterly resent being called unchristian, and like to present themselves as guardians of white Christian civilization.

Professor John Hick of Birmingham – a great champion of harmony between faiths – has written sternly of our church leaders' reluctance specifically to name and oppose such bodies as the National Front. Indeed, he writes, by treating the issue as a controversial matter on which Christians may be expected to differ, they have unwittingly aided the neo-Nazi movements towards the respectability which they covet. Racialism, says John Hick, is not a special subject to be relegated to subcommittees of experts – thus removing it from the churches' main agenda. It is the most obvious violation of Christian faith today.

Professor Hick, of course, is not alone in wishing to see the churches excommunicate what he calls the neo-Nazis with full ritual of bell, book and candle, live and in colour at peak viewing time. Nevertheless, the Community and Race Relations Unit of the British Council of Churches (yes, one of those expert subcommittees) pleads not guilty on behalf of the church leaders. There's hardly a synod, a bishop or a Moderator in the land who does not stand solemnly committed to some resolution or document accepting a multiracial, multicultural Britain and denouncing the National Front and similar bodies as contrary to Christ's commandments.

It would be naïve to pretend that the bishops and Moderators represent the whole-hearted commitment of all the faithful. But I do think it is a weakness of the British Council of Churches' campaign of leaflets and declarations against the Front, that it is hardly a campaign at all. Too much has been devolved: there is no continuing clout behind it. The Council says it is getting back signatures 'in thousands'. How many thousands? 'We're not in the counting game', comes the reply. Well, one knows they are short of money and staff; but it would have been good to know if, say, one in every hundred British Christians who might be counted eligible to sign a declaration had, in fact, done so. (*Later: The B.C.C. claimed upwards of 200,000 signatures.*)

I'm well aware that the statement that 'racism is unchristian' does not go unchallenged in itself. The significance of Noah's curse on the sons of Ham has been explained to me by experts like Governors George Wallace and Orval Faubus – way down south in Dixie. And there's a lady in Southall who keeps quoting to me from Ezra 9 and 10 and (rather curiously) Jude verse 7. She also sends me leaflets from Pretoria. But I don't find they stand up well against the Gospel of loving one's neighbour, or against the leadership of Christians I've known and respected like Harry Morton, Colin Morris, Trevor Huddleston and Martin Luther King. And if middle-aged, middle-class men like these sound too trendy-left, the finest theological case I have heard for accepting and defending the new black presence in Britain was put by that least trendy of prelates, Graham Leonard of Truro.

You might add to that a diocesan letter by the Bishop of Durham, John Habgood. It is by no means without understanding for those who find their way of life affronted by strangers. But the bishop lays it down firmly that racism is a matter of finding a scapegoat and exploiting our hankering for an enemy. And at this point, Bishop Habgood points as accusingly at the virulent anti-Fascists as he does at the National Front. It is hatred and violence, not party labels, that constitute wickedness; and there is a potential Nazi – or, I suppose, a Fascist-basher – in each of us. It is up to each of us to fight that in ourselves.

Only Human Nature

4 March 1978

What to do when tortured: (1) Should you be released after torture, go immediately to a doctor and get his report on you, with photographs if possible. (2) Now go and visit a lawyer and instruct him to sue the minister responsible. (3) Under torture, always tell the truth and nothing else. If you are tortured beyond endurance and sign an untrue statement, this will make things more difficult when you come to court. (4) If you have been maltreated and are not released, you should demand to see a doctor or magistrate. You should also try to memorize the names and descriptions of the people torturing you. (5) If it is not possible for you to bring evidence to a court, visit your priest or pastor and ask him to write down everything that happened to you.

Well, that was my summary of one of the most astonishing pastoral letters of this gruesome age. It was issued jointly to their congregations by the leaders of the Anglican, Roman Catholic and Evangelical Lutheran churches in Namibia, south-west Africa. And it was promptly banned by the South African authorities.

It has reached me as part of a report entitled *Torture – A Cancer in Our Society*, which was prepared in Namibia by a Roman Catholic priest (Father Heinz Hunke) and an Anglican lay worker named Justin Ellis. They are both still in residence there. Banned again by the South Africans, their report has now been published in Britain by the Catholic Institute for International Relations and the British Council of Churches. Its main assertion is that systematic torture has become 'institutionalized' in Namibia – a routine part of the system of what is officially called 'law and order'. If so, it says, that system which claims its legitimacy as Western, democratic and Christian is just another form of barbarism.

As evidence for their assertion, the authors submit a dozen sworn affidavits by African victims of alleged torture. Not one of them was actually charged with a crime. All of them say they were tortured expertly and obscenely with electric shock – several of them while trussed up and spitted like chickens. Their descriptions, in the plain, unemotional language of courtroom statements, make one almost ashamed to be human – because of the experienced cruelty and relish attributed to the torturers (both white and black).

The report also includes a letter to Father Hunke from Justice M. J. Steyn, the South-African-appointed Administrator-General of Namibia, who says he has carefully investigated the allegations and continues: 'I am satisfied that there is no substance in your averments that assaults upon and the torture of detainees and prisoners have become institutionalized in this territory and condoned even by the Courts of Law. You were undoubtedly ill-served by your informants . . . You can rest assured that I will never tolerate or condone the infliction of unlawful violence upon anybody . . . But individual instances of detainees or prisoners being assaulted or tortured will unfortunately occur from time to time, human nature being what it is. Offenders will be severely dealt with.'

Human nature being what it is – and I must admit, some of my mail has given me a rather authoritarian sample – I have no doubt similar unfortunate occurrences are going on now in just about every continent on the globe. It will indeed be a cause for thanksgiving if the efforts of the Rhodesian church leaders succeed in halting the exchange of atrocities there. But why not condemn the guerrillas – the Communists? Well, when the churches – and the archbishops, bishops and councils which speak for them – feel moved to do so, I shall report that too. The authors of this particular document have this to say: 'We condemn all war-crimes – but this is our Government we are talking about. It is all very well saying a spot of "rough treatment" will save life in the end – but in the *real* end it will destroy society – it will become a routine part of interrogation, not only in security and political cases, but in ordinary crime too. If our own Government condones it, how is it superior to the enemy? How can we claim to be defending civilized Christian humanity?'

You will notice I have allowed the 'we' and 'our' to become ambiguous. For it seems we all have our security problems. And we all have 'human nature' to cope with.

Paranonsense

11 March 1978

We're an odd lot: here we are, with belief in the teachings of the Church going fast downhill – and what's in fashion? Science fiction, occultism, astrology – the so-called 'paranormal'. That Jesus turned water into wine, walked on the waters and rose from the dead is laughed out of court, but an amazing number of people take extrasensory perception, levitation and little green men with the utmost seriousness. The Holy Ghost has fallen on hard times, but spirits and demons are big business.

The Church is bound to be somewhat embarrassed by all this, because although the last thing it wants is to be identified with necromancy and pagan sorcery, there's no denying that the Bible is full of events beyond our normal comprehension. And the Church still takes account of that. In spite of the objections of many eminent theologians, the Church of England has recently overhauled its machinery for the administration and control of exorcism.

But the point I was originally making was aimed at secular hypocrisy rather than religious. It seems to me a great deal easier for believers to take the unusual in their stride than for unbelievers to do so. God moves in a mysterious way, we confess: we do not expect to understand the how or why of everything. The people who've got problems are the ruthlessly scientific – or perhaps I should say, the relentlessly materialist.

Time was when all reasonable people believed in the unreasonable – accepted the power of witches, possession by devils and the influence of the stars. I suppose the relentlessly materialist would say now that the last three or four centuries have only proved how wrong such people were, and, they argue, the next three or four centuries will surely help to extend the territories of reason. I can see no Christian point in deploring this. Understanding the laws of astronomy doesn't make the starry skies any the less marvellous, and if one day we understand how faith-healing happens we will surely not be any the less thankful for it. I'm pretty sure, however, that we will never get to the bottom of *everything* – for, as we push on with our explanations, the universe seems simultaneously to get bigger and bigger at one end, smaller and smaller at the other – receding infinitely and becoming less and less 'material'.

The believer, surely, must trust that in some sense the paranormal is perfectly normal – or at least, not arbitrary. There is a reason for it somewhere, and a good reason. I am not one of those who is seized with terror at the thought that the universe may contain principles beyond my control or understanding or prediction. What worries me about the current wave of interest in odd phenomena – (and can it really be true, by the way, that the United Nations is to investigate flying saucers?) – what worries me is twofold. First, the diversion of time, talent and money from really urgent needs like cyclone relief and prayer. And alongside this is the quite extraordinary unimportance – the triviality, even – of most of the events held out to us as paranormal.

I admit to being a professional sceptic (which is not, by the way, the same as being a cynic). It may be that I'm completely lacking in psychic sensitivity – although I would claim to have quite frequent (how shall I put it?) apprehensions of the transcendent. But I spend a good deal of time in a part of west Cornwall which *ought* to be saturated in spookiness – and yet I find it perfectly benign. Nothing paranormal has ever happened to me in fifty years, and frankly I'm quite glad to have been spared such experiences, because most of them (if not quite all) seem to be a waste of time. If there is anything in astrology, why aren't astrologers running the world by now? If we *are* being visited by beings from outer space, why don't they stop fooling about and do something either devastating or constructive? If we *can* get in touch with the dead, why do they utter such platitudes? And if Mr Uri Geller really *has* these astonishing powers, why can't he find something better to do than bend spoons with them? Far from being terrified by the paranormal, I find myself, at best, mildly amused. Compared with the miracles, majesty and terror of God's ordinary, everyday world, it is frankly disappointing.

Full-time Fathers

18 March 1978

Under the rather dreary title of *Theological Training and the Theological Colleges*, the bishops of the Church of England have hoisted what they hope will prove a banner of confidence – something around which the Church can halt its retreat, rally, and at length advance again. It is, in fact, a set of thirteen resolutions welcoming the recent increase in the number of men accepted for training for the full-time ordained ministry, and promising support for the fourteen theological colleges that train them: at first for three years, rolling forward an additional twelve months every year, provided the number of acceptable candidates does not decline.

At the moment that number is rising: it shot up from 250 in 1976 to 350 last year, and the bishops would be happy to see it reach 450 a year before long – even without the admission of women candidates. The current strength of the priesthood in the field is about 11,000, but this is bound to go on falling in the early 1980s because so many priests are now in their sixties and seventies. Nor can there be any immediate end to the merging of parishes and closing of redundant churches. It would be rash to promise more than a slowing down and flattening out of the curve of decline for a few years yet.

Behind the bishops' document there lies what you might call 'Coggan's Counter-offensive': the conviction that it is time to spread the Word, banish the defeatism that has crept into the Church, and to reaffirm that the Church of England is the nation-wide network of parishes, staffed by full-time ministers, and shall remain so. In the past, morale has been badly shaken, not only by declining attendances, financial alarms, shifting doctrines and liturgies, and the loss of functions to the State, but by a confusing variety of plans like the Sheffield Report which have left priests, congregations and colleges alike feeling uncertain and insecure. What the bishops hope to do now is to nail down a reasonably long-term policy and get the Synod to underwrite it. Indeed one reason why this could mark the turning of the tide is that there are signs the tide is already turning – not least the readiness of diocesan synods, when faced with a demanding budget, to dig down and find the money.

And money will have to be found to train, house, pay and pension the new recruits, and to do so adequately (as the bishops urge). At the heart of this rallying call – in which it is not hard to hear the insistent voice of Archbishop Coggan – lies the principle that there is no substitute after all for the full-time stipendiary parish priest. The ministry of the Church of England is not to be allowed to lapse into a part-time hobby. I am sure the bishops would want to add here that their aim is a *varied* ministry – and the more working priests, auxiliaries, deaconesses and lay workers there are, the better: but not at the expense of the seven-days-a-week vicar.

Of course a bishop *would* say that, wouldn't he? There *are* Christians who challenge the need for full-time priests, or indeed priests at all, and would claim that the Church only departed from the truth when it fell into the hands of organized professionals. However, it has to be admitted such people are in the minority. Most anticlericalists end up with no church and no Christianity at all.

It may very well be that what the Church of England (like other churches) has been suffering from is really a lack of confidence, and that the best way to renew it is to inject it with keen new priests who will revive its congregations. But it seems to me there are certain details that do need pondering. For a start, these will have to be really outstanding people – not just pious and well-intentioned.

Stipends and pensions may not be everything, but they could be better – and so could the various back-up services the clergy need. Above all, can the Church reach and attract such people in terms of making up its mind what it is calling them *to*? How does a congregation really regard its priest: as a man of prayer and worship, a free-lance social worker, a leader, a teacher, or a status symbol who mustn't make a nuisance of himself? Brutally, does it really want him? Will it support him? Does it really have a role for him and the faith he stands for? If not, all this is hollow.

The Degradation of the Cross

25 March 1978

I was reading the other day that 'Jesus was a typical prisoner of conscience – arrested, tortured and executed "in the name of the people" (as they always say) – the classic fate of a man who threatens the Establishment'.

This, I am sure, is a vivid and valid way of asserting the relevance of the crucifixion to our own times. The world is full of such 'prisoners of conscience', from Chile to Cuba, from Cape Town to Kiev. And yet I think it is important that we should not make the mistake of assessing the crucifixion too much in modern terms. In saying this, I am not worried about protecting Jesus's special position as Son of God: that, in some sense, emerges *from* the crucifixion. What I want to do first is to emphasize the very deliberate horror and degradation of the way he died – something to which there is really no parallel today.

Thanks in part to the painters of the Italian Renaissance, we tend to visualize the crucifixion as a kind of frozen operatic tableau or wall-painting, with the characters arranged in decorative attitudes, decorously draped, and scarcely suffering at all. For who could bear to live with the truth – that crucifixion was no mere style of execution, it was a long-drawn-out method of torturing people to death in public? And Jesus suffered a death that was not only extremely painful and disgusting, but was also reserved exclusively for slaves and traitors. It was specifically designed to make a horrible example of the victim – to humiliate him to the depths, destroy all traces of human dignity in him, and deter anyone else from following his lead. If we examine classical literature, we find that while torture was extensive in the Roman world, nice people regarded it with nausea. Cicero wrote: 'The very name of the cross should never come near the person of a Roman citizen, nor even enter his thoughts, his sight or his hearing.' In a world ruled by terror, it was seen as a necessary obscenity for keeping the mass of slaves and subject peoples under Roman control. Indeed it was known to be so degrading that until the Emperor Constantine substituted hanging as the State penalty, Christians could not bring themselves to portray the crucifixion itself in their art.

St Paul describes the cross as a stumbling-block to the Jews and folly to the Greeks. Again, we tend to overlook why. The Jewish stumbling-block goes back to Deuteronomy – where it is written that the body of an executed criminal hanging on the tree brings the curse of God upon the land, and must be buried before nightfall. So how could God have, as his divine Son, a being who was by God's own law accursed? The Holy One *could not* be implicated in such alien blasphemy. As for the Greeks, they knew perfectly well that the gods were immortal. It was the sheerest folly to try and preach them a dead god, or one who (even if he did rise again from the tomb) had permitted himself such undignified suffering. (A half-hearted way round this is what is known as Docetism – the theory that only a shadow of Jesus hung on the cross. But that is not the Gospel witness: indeed the whole point is that it is not.)

What St Paul is saying, then, is that whether you are trying to sell the good news of Jesus to Jews or to Greeks, you have got a superficially most unattractive product on your hands: a god who is accursed, unclean, discredited and dead. The god that St Paul and company were offering was a kind of upside-down, revolutionary god: not a sun king in glory, but (to the disbelieving world) a subhuman, butchered like an animal. And there are various indications that the Roman world did revile and ridicule the Christians for precisely such reasons. And remember, in those days, public cruelty was an entertainment.

All this we tend to lose sight of. Today we do not openly torture people to death as a public spectacle. When we do torture them, it is done furtively, in private, with the excuse of 'interrogation', and it is the executioner, not the victim, who is shamed in the eyes of the world. I suggest this is due in no small measure to the influence exerted by the death of Jesus. I also suggest that if we can appreciate the apparently devastating finality of that death, only then can we appreciate the invincible power of whatever it was the disciples experienced in the resurrection.

Catholic Tastes

1 April 1978

This week I'm speaking from the Catholic (or *Anglo*-Catholic as some would prefer it) Renewal Conference which has been going on for the past three days among a thousand delegates at Loughborough University. Although the organizers beg you not to treat it as the High Church reply to last year's whizz-bang Evangelical jamboree at Nottingham, it is impossible not to make some comparisons. Nottingham was a well-prepared exercise in popular manifesto-writing – at which it succeeded admirably. Loughborough is less of a debating chamber – more an act of worship. 'We are not here to make decisions or issue statements,' says Brother Donald, the Franciscan major-domo of the affair, 'and certainly not to stage a "We Hate Women Priests Week".'

Well, maybe not – but there is a profoundly clerical and even celibate air about Loughborough, with monks and nuns much more in evidence, a constant twitching of hands in the sign of the cross, and Roman collars (with only the merest hyphen of white showing) almost *de rigueur*. Here a cape, there a cassock, and speculation in the press-room about when the first biretta would be sighted.

If the Evangelical emphasis is on preaching the Word, that in the Catholic wing is upon celebrating the Eucharist – upon the richness (which is a favourite Catholic term) and magic (which is not) of the sacraments, their rituals and vestments. For all its theatricality (another word that may get me in trouble) it is a tradition which gives worship a much more private air than the 'public meeting' atmosphere of some Evangelical worship. And perhaps this 'privacy' has something to do with the depression which has crept into Anglo-Catholicism during the past ten or fifteen years – a feeling of isolation and lack of leadership which many of the priests I have met at Loughborough seem to hope the conference may remedy. A number of them confess to a great loneliness, as if the Church of England was passing them by.

There are those who believe that if there really *is* a renewal of the Church in this country it will not come from within England at all, but from the United States, the Third World, even the Soviet Union. There is a considerable fascination among Anglo-Catholics with the even richer rituals of the Eastern Orthodox churches (and we all know where *they* stand on women priests . . .).

With Rome there is some disillusion (though not with Cardinal Hume, who is deeply revered). One leading churchman complained to me that Vatican Two had 'pulled out the carpet from under Anglo-Catholicism'. Yet another, even higher up the ecclesiastical tree, speculated that if only Rome would open up its altars and legitimize intercommunion, then (as he put it) within ten years the only people outside the Catholic Church would be the Quakers and the Plymouth Brethren.

This is, of course, a very priestly, sacramental view of what the churches are for; but then the specialness of the priesthood as apostolic guardian and administrator of the sacraments is surely central to the Catholic tradition. It helps to give Loughborough its air of an Old Boys' Reunion (not that the boys are all old – there's a fair sprinkling of bearded young priests as well). On three occasions I have overheard snatches of the ancient view that there are areas of doctrine into which the laity should not needlessly be led: after all, I was told, renewal has always been born among the priesthood.

The modern bad word for this would be 'élitist', I suppose. It certainly risks becoming introspective. Why, for example, has the Catholic wing seemed to have lost that deep social conscience that used to be its speciality? It seemed odd to provide only two hours for what were listed as 'Current Issues' – and for most members to assume that meant women priests. But to be fair, present-day Catholics recognize that both wings are needed – Evangelicals, too – if that ungainly bird the Church of England is to be airborne at all. And I for one would hate to be without such richly Catholic characters as Father Brian Brindley, manipulator of the General Synod, or the cleric who brought his Alsatian dog to the conference, feeding it supper each night on the tail-gate of his station wagon, while refreshing himself from a large brown bottle. Was it he, I wonder, whom I heard in another setting confide to a colleague, 'Of course I am the author of the *definitive* life of St Chad'?

Dirty Work

8 April 1978

I gather – although I have received only one letter referring to it – that last week's note about the Catholic Renewal Conference gave some offence, for which I am sorry. This week, I shall not try to vary the offence by talking about Princess Margaret's divorce (there is precedent even for journalists to keep out of the stone-casting game) but I do feel drawn to talk about pornography. For the Roman Catholic Social Welfare Commission has just published its evidence to the Williams Committee which is reviewing the law on the subject.

Or rather (to quote the official mandate) it is 'to review

the laws concerning obscenity, indecency and violence in publications, displays and entertainments – except in broadcasting'. (The Commission thinks broadcasting *should* be covered.) The inclusion of violence is interesting, not only because it reflects the feeling that violence is at least as dangerous as obscenity, but also because it falls in with the view that, fundamentally, gratuitous representations of lust and violence spring from the same source – the dehumanizing of man and woman which, because we are made by God, is a kind of blasphemy as well as self-destruction.

A few weeks back we had the Bishop of Truro putting the Church of England's views, in evidence that bears comparison with that of the Roman Catholics. The Anglicans are a good deal fussier about distinctions between the erotic, the pornographic and the obscene. They take the view that while erotica *celebrate* sex, pornography trivializes it and obscenity represents a deliberate attempt (sometimes motivated by hatred) to destroy man's essential dignity and humanity. This, as I was trying to say two weeks ago, was precisely the object of crucifixion. And, as another incidental, the emphasis on true, whole humanity as God's design for man is the essential message of the great Swiss theologian, Hans Küng.

The Church of England's evidence goes on to link violence with obscenity. It understands how people can speak of the 'obscenity' of violence and of the 'violence' done to man by depriving him of work or dignity – though I'm glad to see it notes the imprecision this can lead to. Theologians, quite as much as politicians and broadcasters, are open to the dangers of using words sloppily.

The Roman Catholic evidence also keeps 'pornography' and 'representations of violence' in the same yoke, while I think it makes a clearer distinction between them. (I only wish it wouldn't use the dreadful word 'encapsulate' so often.) It makes the same point about the use of either as mere entertainment: that by taking them out of the complete human context, the entertainers trivialize, isolate, dehumanize and distort humanity. The Catholic evidence grants that such representations *may* have the effect of undermining the standards and institutions of society. The Church of England document reveals some perplexity over effects, and would like the research to be clarified, aware that there is much contradiction in it.

At this point the Catholic Commission says frankly that the link between cause and effect depends on disputed evidence and suspect explanatory theories. Most sociological findings are really professions of faith based upon some theory of human nature. And to Catholics, pornography and violence are wrong not because of their supposed effects but because they violate the Christian view of that nature. They are wrong because they are wrong. In any case, they may well be a symptom of the general disease, rather than a cause of it. The two churches join hands then in agreeing that society has a right to set limits to what it will accept in public, and that people are entitled to legal protection from the intrusion of obnoxious material into their lives and that of their immature children.

The Roman Catholics are all for replacing the unworkable definition of obscenity as 'tending to corrupt'. But when it seeks to substitute 'outrage to contemporary standards of humanity accepted by the public at large', well – I wonder. Will a jury be any better at judging outrage? And what standards *are* accepted? Maybe higher than we think. But how to be sure if Christian legislators can't put it on paper?

The Martyrdom of Moro

22 April 1978

The cynical exploitation of Signor Aldo Moro – leader of Italy's Christian Democrats – whatever his ultimate fate, is an affront to the civilization of western Europe – and was intended to be. The challenge, not only to Italian Christians but to all who believe in a humane balance between individual and community is: how do we meet this assault? How do we survive if it happens here? I.R.A.

bombings have already given us part of the answer: we endure, we do not exaggerate or panic or over-react. But what in fact do we do if (say) a member of the royal family, a noted ex-Prime Minister, is kidnapped and tormented in a 'people's prison'?

It seems to me that one thing we must do in advance is to resist – in our schools, our Press and our pulpits – the subversion of our language by terms like 'people's trial' and 'execution by suicide'. Who dares to speak for the people, but the ballot-box? But it is just as dangerous to start using terms like 'law and order' and 'discipline' as excuses for repressing everything that is not well to the right of centre. Whenever extremists intend to treat their fellow humans like animals, they begin by re-classifying them as sub-human. And if you believe we are all made a little lower than the angels and crowned with glory – that is blasphemy.

But as I think I've said before, loving our enemies has to mean listening to them, even when they say things we would rather not hear. The Red Brigade, the Baader-Meinhoff gang and the I.R.A. Provisionals talk a kind of gobbledegook which is actually intended to shut their own members in and the rest of us out – like one of those secret languages that children use. It may even be paranoid, but behind it has to lie something, some hurt, some frustration, some injustice, and it is only practical to find out what that is. A church that is really attentive to the young, the poor, the disadvantaged ought to know. Which is why – however leftish they may sound – some of the Roman Catholic missionaries in Southern Africa and Latin America are well worth listening to. So are some of our own urban clergy. Prophecy – by which I do not mean using the Old Testament like *Old Moore's Almanack* – is one of the neglected functions of the Church.

But to revert to the fate of Signor Moro – not even the first of its kind – this isn't the place to lecture the authorities about controlling firearms and taking other precautions; but it may be a good moment for public and police alike to reflect on the old-fashioned virtue of honesty. If terrorism strikes here, police and public are going to need each other's confidence and loyalty. A corrupt public has weakened its own defences. A corrupt police force will not be trusted, will not get the co-operation it must have in securing information and denying shelter to the terrorists. The churches could help to bridge the confidence gap – if there is one.

But again, what do we actually do if top rank kidnappings catch on here? It seems to me – though this is much easier to say in the abstract than it would be of a particular case with a name to it – that those on the side of Christian civilization have to be ready to stand up and take casualties. We can't surrender every time, even to save a loved and respected human life. Martyrdom is a word to use sparingly. But we should hold Signor Moro in our prayers today. We have no right to speak over the heads of the victims and their families, and one shudders to think of the tortures and degradation they may have to endure. But, to speak bluntly, God finds replacements for all of us in the end. It may be that those who serve democracy as politicians or public officials may now have to contemplate death as part of their service – and see to it that they are prepared to face it. If so, the rest of us had better start treating them with a new respect and sympathy. There is a very ancient Christian precedent for this kind of sacrifice.

Arms and the Church

29 April 1978

Late next month, there's to be a special session of the United Nations General Assembly to discuss disarmament. The British Council of Churches has called on its members to pray for it. The Roman Catholic bishops have issued a joint pastoral letter about it. The World Council of Churches has been holding a preparatory conference at Montreux. And yet, among the public at large, one detects either apathy or cynicism. What can Christians – and Jews, Sikhs, Hindus and Muslims, for that matter – do about it?

Perhaps we had better begin by deciding if we really believe in disarmament. There is a case to be made for Britain rearming. It's argued that our forces are so run down they don't deter anybody any more. I suppose that could turn us into the first really harmless member of NATO – but only by default, and not because we had deliberately chosen some other active path to peace.

There is increasing interest among the churches in overhauling the old doctrine that some wars are just. There is some movement, especially among Catholics, I find, towards Christian pacifism and positive non-violence. But it has yet to make much headway in the world of politics. Even those who think Britain should take the risk of total disarmament – instead of the risk of being armed to the teeth – are inclined to excuse the so-called liberation movements of the oppressed: which enables other people to point out that one man's liberation movement is another man's terrorism, and are we really going to lay ourselves open to blackmail by criminals? A good question. And are we, in our desperation for jobs, happy with the argument that if we don't sell arms to China and Iran, somebody else will? Is that a Christian way to earn a living?

Yet the pure pacifist approach does require much more thinking, training and mass conversion than has so far been done. It was right of the Roman Catholic bishops to urge support for peace organizations, and centres for peace studies – like that at Bradford.

In the Middle Ages the Church made a very positive contribution by insisting upon certain rules of warfare, even banning certain weapons. There was to be no fighting at week-ends or on saints' days – no destruction of the fruits of the earth or slaughter of innocent peasants. By no means did it always work. Pagans were excluded from its benefits. But there was a certain restraint about warfare and a sense of honour that lasted well into the nineteenth century. It has now vanished – abandoned (during the Second World War) as brutally by Christian countries as by barbarians. Alas, the concept of Christendom, upon which the restraints depended, has been outflanked. But perhaps the churches and the United Nations could try to restore and enforce some sort of rules of warfare once again. And if there are to be weapons, could not each country's needs be assessed, licensed and audited by the U.N.? Could not the U.N. have its own network of spy-in-the-sky satellites, monitoring the whole world and publishing the results?

That isn't my own idea – it came out of the World Council of Churches' conference. That conference laid its hand firmly on the central menace of arms development – for even without war, this process is stripping God's world of its resources, squandering the time, money and talents of some of his cleverest people, and beggaring those nations least able to afford the product. New weapons are being developed, said the conference, not because of military need, but as the result of sheer ingenuity. They are now appearing at a prodigious rate, often frustrating slow-moving disarmament negotiations by altering the whole problem. The United States and Russia (as an Indian delegate put it) 'are riding the nuclear tiger, and don't know how to dismount'.

No need to waste time damning the neutron bomb as such. It was just another example of the military-industrial-scientific-bureaucratic complex pressing forward because it doesn't know how to stand still. Perhaps the world churches have something to say to the U.N. about stillness.

A Tale of Two Irelands

6 May 1978

I'm speaking today from Belfast, towards the end of one of those lightning tours of Ireland that must make the Irish wince. For here comes another 'instant expert'.

It's by no means my first visit, so I should know enough to be cautious. The very language is full of code words and booby traps. Nevertheless, I believe that everybody over in Britain would benefit from a spell here. For the way Ireland is, is very much our responsibility – more especially that of the English and Scots who colonized the place in the past, leaving it with a settler problem not unlike Rhodesia's – though we have a dishonest habit of letting all that slip our memories. We would rather, it seems, worry about Rhodesia.

I began my visit in Dublin – notable today for its terrible prices, its building boom and its suspiciously large Russian Embassy. One hears the occasional complaint of discrimination against Protestants in the South, but in general they seem to be sharing amply in the prosperity that has come upon the Republic thanks to E.E.C. farm prices.

Everyone outside the Republic is convinced it's the Roman Catholic hierarchy that really runs the country. True, there's what you might call a 'special relationship' – as you might expect in a country which is so heavily and devoutly Catholic, and which does care about moral standards in a way some of the rest of us are beginning to envy. But I can only record that senior members of the hierarchy insisted to me they were *not* trying to run the country, and would be glad to see a further separation of Church and State. It seems a pity that Irish politicians do not seem inclined to clarify the constitutional position of a united Ireland. It might make dealings with the North, and the contemplation there of an Irish identity, much easier.

The Anglican Church of Ireland, with its membership on both sides of the border and its Broad Church traditions, already sees itself as a potential bridge between the two societies. To some, this will suggest that the ultimate solution will be a united Ireland, and in fact very few of the various church leaders I've spoken to questioned that. But they didn't question, either, that the Protestant majority in the North won't stand for it now, and cannot possibly be coerced. So the impression I've received is that a united Ireland is inevitable, that it must come gradually, but that 'gradual' must not be an excuse for doing nothing, and that the churches have a vital role to play in helping their people along the many steps that will have to be taken.

It's been said often enough that religion isn't the cause of Ireland's troubles. All the same, it can't be disentangled from them. I've heard it described as a cowboys and Indians situation, with each side wearing its religion as a badge of identity. More than that – each religion does represent a distinctive racial culture.

The Protestant churches have put together thoughtful and constructive documents explaining all this, and organizations like the Quakers and the Corymeela Community have been working for years bringing Catholics and Protestants together, so that they can discover the 'other side' consists of human beings and not animals. The Irish problem is a strange mixture of slow motion and urgency: it's in the long run that such activities will bear fruit.

But what now? I said to begin with that the English ought to visit Ireland more often, then they might begin to understand how insensitive we often seem to both communities – swinging between boredom and brutality, lacking either tact or patience or subtlety – determined only not to lose face. And I think it would do many southern Catholics equal good to come up here to Belfast and to make some effort to understand the Scots-Ulsterman and his identity. The Protestant slogan 'No Surrender' is right in one sense: a new Ireland cannot possibly be built by conquest, but only by honesty. And if politicians dare not take the plunge, why not the churches? All of them.

The Holy Island

27 May 1978

I've confessed before that sacraments aren't my cup of tea, but I do have a taste for holy places. They are the doorways between heaven and Earth – doorways that have been unlocked for us, in nearly every case, by a particular person – and then the way to it endorsed by the feet, knees and lips of countless pilgrims.

I've just been to such a place: Lindisfarne, or Holy Island, off the Northumberland coast. It's not a bit difficult to reach – just five miles off the A1 (M) south of Berwick, and then, if the tide is out, you drive over a tarmacked causeway on to the island itself. The northern part is all sand-dunes, but the south has sheep-pastures, a small fishing harbour, and a village with pubs and souvenir shops and a few places to stay. It can be very, very windy – and I strongly suspect it's the wind of the Holy Spirit, hurling itself against the follies of unbelief.

Beside the village and a spectacular little castle, there also stand the chewed ruins of a Norman priory – all gnawed and gnarled by the elements – and an ageless parish church, where the office is still said daily by the vicar, Denis Bill – though sometimes he has to shout to make himself heard above the howling of the gales. Heard, because he is never alone. Quite apart from the islanders – who, I suspect, take the holiness of their island pretty much for granted – there is always someone in retreat or on pilgrimage in the Church House which can take up to twenty people, on an entirely ecumenical basis. There's someone there at the moment pondering the Sufis, and parties of Roman Catholics use it, too.

This particular doorway to heaven was opened by a most unjustly forgotten man, for, as Bishop Lightfoot of Durham remarked, 'Not Augustine, but Aidan is the true apostle of England'. Aidan came here from Iona in the year 635, at the request of his old schoolfriend King Oswald and founded a community on the Celtic pattern – a monastery that looked simultaneously outward and inward – inward to an intense spiritual life of the most rigorous and eremitical sort – outward in service and mission to the common people. Lindisfarne became a training centre for missionaries who ultimately spread as far south as the Thames – men loved and respected for their poverty and sincerity. The King once gave Aidan a horse – which he promptly disposed of to the first beggar he met. He preferred travelling on foot, for that was how he met the people.

Not long after Aidan came St Cuthbert – the lives of both are well documented by chroniclers like the Venerable Bede. Cuthbert's fame was, if anything, even greater. You might call him the Northumbrian St Francis for his love of birds and beasts, his modesty and his mortification of the flesh. Cuthbert was caught up in the collision between the Celtic tradition and the Roman, a clash that focused upon trivialities like the styles of monkish haircut and the dates of Easter, but was more likely to do with central discipline over heresy. The Celtic church was actually the older in these islands, and I can't help feeling sentimental about it. However, that's academic now. Rome won at Whitby in A.D. 664, and Cuthbert played a leading part in reconciling the two churches. They made him Bishop of Hexham but he cleverly swapped the position with the incumbent of his beloved Lindisfarne. Not that he shirked his missionary duties. There are numerous tales of his teaching and healing. But towards the end of his life he returned to his hermitage and died there as he had lived – cut off by storm and with only five onions to eat.

A century after his death, the first of the Danish raids devastated Lindisfarne. Cuthbert's body, together with the bones of Oswald and Aidan, set off on two centuries of wandering that brought them finally to Durham. At least three times – the latest in 1539 – the coffin was opened and Cuthbert's body found to be supple and uncorrupted – a sure sign of sainthood. To most people, Holy Island is best known today for the superb illuminated gospels that it produced, but I assure you, its spiritual powers remain. It preserves the simplicity and the passionate rigours of the saints who opened its door to the winds of the Spirit.

Till What do us Part?

3 June 1978

I commend to anyone concerned about family morals the Church of England report, *Marriage and the Church's Task* – and, by way of a supplement, the parallel document issued by the Anglo-Catholic Church Union, *The Theology and Meaning of Marriage*. Inevitably they have both been described as 'divorce reports', and after all, this is where they *do* touch the lives of many ordinary people. But, as I hope to show, what they are really about is that abused and neglected institution – the family. Perhaps it ought not to be necessary to explain why the family is the Church's business, but I think it is worth suggesting that when it urges something as God's will for us – like a stable family – the Church should really be pointing us not into some area of abstract theology that it has got itself trapped in, but towards our true, God-given nature. For as Hans Küng says, God wills our welfare, not our misery.

Both these reports accept – as surely any reader of the Bible must – that the early Church saw the commands of the Lord as forbidding divorce and remarriage, among its members. Mind you, it isn't quite as simple as that. What about the exception in St Matthew – which the Protestant and Orthodox churches interpret as allowing divorce on the grounds of adultery? And was Jesus claiming to brush aside Deuteronomy and the rest of the Mosaic law? All the same, it is fair enough to say 'Jesus was against divorce'.

The High doctrine of marriage goes on to say that because of this, because the grace of sacrament is bestowed, 'signifying the mystical union that is betwixt Christ and his Church', and because marriage becomes 'a great ladder of spirituality based upon our physical nature', the very possibility of divorce is the negation of Christian marriage, and to pretend that its vows can be renewed in different circumstances would be for the Church to weaken its witness to the glory of marriage.

I know lay people who say all this is a lot of priestly mumbo-jumbo – and often celibate mumbo-jumbo at that. A more moderate view comes from the majority on the official commission, who take the view that certainly divorce ought to be exceptional, and thus remarriage too, and the best way of maintaining high standards is to marry and remarry within the Church.

Now the 'indissoluble' view of marriage is not just a rigidly Scriptural view, it is a profoundly sacramental one, and I doubt if there can be any shaking that. It's no good saying 'What God hath joined is one thing – what the Reverend John Brown hath joined may be quite another'. One might ask: but shouldn't the Church be giving sinners a second chance – isn't it neglecting its mission by being so exclusive? And what attraction can it offer to thousands who nowadays simply live together: has it written them off? As for Scripture, wasn't the early Church expecting the end of the world at any minute? All of this, I am sure, the 'indissoluble' school would patiently reject. I do not suppose they would be impressed by what three Anglican clergymen have told me – that in their experience, second marriages of divorced people are usually deeply Christian and spiritual as never before.

It has been said that it's not a matter of making divorce easier, but marriage more difficult. Personally, I don't think people do undertake church weddings so lightly. Or divorce, either. Who knows what agonies are suffered in private? But surely one of the great strengths of a church wedding is that it commits two whole families to the support of the marriage. It should be, in every sense, a family affair. And the main report is quite right, in my view, in denouncing successive Governments for their total lack of interest in sustaining the family and marriage, and for failing to recognize how they have been battered and shattered by public policy. Housing is an obvious example; inflation that drives people out to work too hard; and taxation that actually penalizes regular marriage. Should there not be a special allowance for the mother who stays at home to bring up her children? Or don't Governments care about our collapsing birth rate? Perhaps the churches will show that *they* do.

Theo-science and Sci-faith

10 June 1978

Before I return to the subject of religion and science I had better apologize to the lady who has complained of my being too 'highbrow'. Believe me, my mind has been officially certified by the university as second-class, but it can easily make out the significance of a report from the British Association entitled *The Sensitive Scientist.* The point this is trying to make is that scientists are not *in*-sensitive to the social and moral implications of what they do. Traditionally, they have dedicated themselves to the pursuit of knowledge for its own sake, regardless of consequences, and from this have followed commandments to cherish complete truthfulness, defend freedom of enquiry, publish discoveries openly and so on. But these offer little guidance on matters like weapons research, experiments with animals, waste and pollution. For science involves more than a search for knowledge (it is argued) – it is a social activity, and so we get conflicting values which have to be weighed in the balance against one another, and not all such conflicts can easily be resolved.

Last year, a select group of Canadians met in Ontario under the chairmanship of our own Dr Magnus Pyke. Their deliberations, like those of the British Association group, were spurred on by the churches and both scientists and theologians took part. Their objective? To find out what theology might have to say to science in the search for (excuse the North American gobbledegook) 'global macro-ethics'.

There was a previous attempt at this a few years back in Bucharest, and once again there was a certain 'dialogue of the deaf' about it all. Dr Pyke, who might be described nowadays as a spiritual free-lance, adopted a classic position: that science and theology pursue different aims, ascertain their truths by different methods, and (I quote) 'that natural knowledge is ethically neutral'.

This, of course, sends a shudder up the spines of people who worry about fast breeder-reactors, genetic engineering and vivisection. According to the published report – which has just been issued by the United Church of Canada – the symposium refuted Dr Pyke's view and encouraged the idea that science and theology might become allies in shaping this 'global ethical system'. But I must say I have a good deal of sympathy with Dr Pyke. I do not think that religion and science are enemies, but it might be positively dangerous for them to attempt a coalition. Science monitored and guided by the Church into a series of crusades? I hope not.

Not that a coalition is really possible. Dr Pyke was actually shocked to meet theologians who were 'trying to be technicians', as he put it. Surely a basic reason for the incompatibility of the two is that they are using language in totally different ways. Science uses it practically, to describe things that can be measured and experimented with. Theology uses language poetically, metaphysically, to describe things that *cannot* be measured. And surely science is impersonal. A piece of science does not express the scientist, but every piece of theology expresses the theologian. To say that science can be morally committed is a sort of pathetic fallacy, like saying an oak-tree rejoices at the spring. Yet of course scientists can have moral commitments – should be socially and ethically concerned. Am I splitting hairs here? I think not, because I believe this is an important distinction, emphasizing *personal* responsibility, underlining that science – as a body and system of knowledge – cannot incorporate an ethical system or religion.

Ethics are constantly being affected by social, political and economic factors. But I think it is also important to say that religion is about much more than ethics: it is about salvation, worship and the whole meaning of life. A religious scientist may act differently from one who is not, and a theologian who understands science may (like Professor Thomas Torrance or Teilhard de Chardin) obtain new insights. But heaven preserve us from theo-science or sci-faith! Surely there are believing scientists who use language one way in church on Sundays, and quite another way in the laboratory on Mondays, without being hypocrites. Wisdom lies in drawing the distinction.

Rigour, Hardness and Austerity

24 June 1978

I've just been at a conference of religious broadcasters – held in an abandoned nunnery near St Albans, the ground floor of which (when I left) had been given over to Mr James Mason and others, making a kind of Sherlock Holmes horror film.

On the upper floors we had more serious business. In particular, we had Miss Marghanita Laski – probably the most sharp-edged speaker I know, unashamedly élitist – talking to us about religious broadcasting for the unbeliever. It put us very much to the test, and (speaking for myself) I am not sure I passed with very good marks.

Miss Laski has no doubt at all that religious broadcasting has a valid purpose: it is to guide people towards the satisfaction of the most basic inner needs – needs which are felt by everyone with any degree of seriousness at all – and which are expressed in the Christian reference to the communion of saints, the forgiveness of sins, the resurrection of the body and the life everlasting. We must all allow for the irrational, says Miss Laski, and at no time is that more clear than at a funeral. She herself would settle happily for the service of the Church of England.

But where Miss Laski finds herself in disagreement with what she hears on the air is in the matter of morals. Here, she thinks, the hungry sheep look up and are not fed. The whole philosophy of 'judge not that ye be not judged' has been taken too far. The substitution of generalized love for judgement has done the community infinite harm, she believes. We overlook the Stoic value of endurance.

Among the subjects she would like to hear discussed

more are honour and duty: the sense of honour to keep one's word, the duty of parents and children, husbands and wives to one another, and the mutual duties of trade-unionists and employers. She is also concerned about the permissive philosophy that love – sexual love – justifies all kinds of cruelty to others.

No doubt you've already concluded, as I have, that this is old-fashioned (no harm in that), Victorian, even puritan morality, with little or nothing in it that Mr Muggeridge or Mrs Whitehouse could not applaud. Is there no such thing as moral repulsion left, demands Miss Laski? Some of us are drawn to hardness, rigour and austerity. 'I would like to see,' she adds, 'your religious broadcasting so disturbing that no one with guts could ignore it.' Perhaps I should add here that a few hours earlier we had heard a Jesuit speaker, John Harriott, declare: '*Real* religious programmes should leave blood on the floor', and call for broadcasting by 'poets, obsessives and mystical explorers'.

And there, I suspect, is the catch. I can imagine the cheers that greeted that call for plain speaking on honour and duty would turn to howls at the discovery that it really *was* disturbing – really *did* leave blood on the floor. Two or three morally obsessed and poetical *Yours Faithfullies* would probably be the end of my career. Not that I couldn't write them – *if* I had a mind to start judging people instead of trying to understand them and pass their messages on to each other, which I think is what I'm meant to be doing. To quote the head of German T.V. (Channel 2): 'The presence of things Christian in the media cannot be greater than the actual presence of Christianity in our society. Broadcasters are not the extended arm of the Church. They should not confuse the microphone with the pulpit.'

They do, of course. I do, from time to time. But I doubt if it's very much use. Anyone, believer or unbeliever, can have high morals. Christianity, Judaism and other faiths too are about a good deal more. They are about glory and worship and oneness and salvation, too. Some people, like Marghanita Laski, say they get that component from music and art – though I was glad to hear Miss Laski draw a firm line between art and religion. It may well be that we have all gone too far in saying people's private lives are their own, though if we are going to intervene in them more, I hope we shall tread with care. For Christians, surely, love (and I don't mean erotic love) is more important than rigour, hardness and austerity, which can hide a terrible selfishness and cruelty of their own.

The Prince and the Prelates

8 July 1978

An occasional function of royalty is to drop bricks into stagnant water – and that's what Prince Charles has done in his brief excursion as the plain man's theologian. I hope I needn't rehearse what he said at too great a length. Addressing the centenary rally of the Salvation Army, he praised it for its lack of involvement in academic dogma, and said it was 'worse than folly' that at a time like this, when people were perplexed about right and wrong, Christians should still be arguing about doctrinal matters which could only bring needless distress to a considerable number of people. A day later, the Press decided the Prince was talking about the Pope's refusal of a church wedding to Prince Michael of Kent and his bride. The text hardly proves that *was* in his mind; nevertheless, it leapt to the mind of the Roman Catholic Archbishop of Glasgow, Thomas Winning, who took off after the Prince and landed a number of punches: (1) The Prince was encouraging 'woolly' Christianity. (2) Millions of Catholics who cared deeply about their doctrine would be offended. (3) The point of doctrine was to give people certainty about right and wrong. And (4) What about the scandal of denying the throne to Roman Catholics?

There followed a polite counter-attack from the Archbishop of York and the retiring President of the Methodist Conference – who unlike Archbishop Winning were actually present at the rally – arguing that no one who heard the context thought the Prince was attacking Rome and trying to shift attention rather to the scandal of doctrinal bickering, which, they said, many in the Church had been deploring for a long time past. I doubt, though, if this statement appeased Roman Catholics much by its reference to 'a seeming preoccupation with relatively unimportant matters'. No way, surely, to speak of papal infallibility, or the validity of Anglican orders.

It is not difficult to shoot holes in what Prince Charles said – or rather, what he is *thought* to have said. It's true that the Salvation Army steers clear of sacraments and priesthood, but it has a 190-page *Handbook of Doctrine* (including the Nicene Creed), and when it comes to marriage, its rules are extremely rigid. So, for that matter, are those of the Church of England, which bickers as much as anyone.

There are, I think, two points to be made about Roman Catholics and the throne. At first sight, their exclusion *is* unfair. But until the Church of England is disestablished, the monarch remains its governor and has to uphold the Thirty-nine Articles. You couldn't even *ask* a Roman Catholic to do that, surely. Next, the Bishop of Worcester may well be right – if regrettably so – when he says people are not ready for a Roman Catholic monarch. I think millions of non-churchgoers still regard the Church of England as their national church, and would be unhappy at the idea of their monarch kneeling at any other altar. It may be hypocritical, but there it is, I'm afraid.

Prince Charles thought what we ought to be worried about was whether people were becoming atheists – their ideas of right and wrong, things of the spirit, the meaning and beauty of nature – and here I think he truly reflected the religious instincts of very many people – instincts that often feel fettered in church, yet are sadly wasted outside. But doctrine does matter to serious Christians, and the centuries have shown, 'No dogma – no Church'; and if there *is* bickering (there is much less than there used to be), it is a product now of efforts to come together. I have to say here that I'm not speaking for myself, for it seems to me that in trying to capture the uncatchable, the churches have made too tight a net of too coarse a fibre. I am enchanted by the vision of Graham Dowell, Vicar of Hampstead, who dreams of a coming great church that will combine Eastern Orthodox intensity with Quaker openness to the Spirit. (A tall order, though.)

The theology of the plain man may be over-simple: there is more to religion than music and nature and decent behaviour. But, equally, religion is too important to be left to bishops. I say three cheers for Prince Charles for reminding the churches what fools they can look to a large part of the nation.